COOK SMART vegetarian

Delicious, easy vegetarian recipes for all occasions,
all with *ProPoints* values

SIMON &
SCHUSTER
ILLUSTRATED

London · New York · Sydney · Toronto

A CBS COMPANY

First published in Great Britain by Simon & Schuster UK Ltd, 2011
A CBS Company

Copyright © 2011, Weight Watchers International, Inc.
Simon & Schuster Illustrated Books, Simon & Schuster UK Ltd, First Floor, 222 Gray's Inn Road, London WC1X 8HB

Weight Watchers, **ProPoints** and the **ProPoints** icon are the registered trademarks of Weight Watchers International Inc. and are used under license by Simon & Schuster UK Ltd.

Weight Watchers Publications: Jane Griffiths, Donna Watts, Imogen Prescott, Nina McKerlie and Selina Kaushal.

Recipes written by: Sue Ashworth, Sue Beveridge, Tamsin Burnett-Hall, Cas Clarke, Siân Davies, Roz Denny, Becky Johnson, Kim Morphew, Joy Skipper, Penny Stephens and Wendy Veale.

Photography by: Iain Bagwell, Steve Baxter, Steve Lee and Juliet Piddington.
Design and typesetting by Tiger Media Ltd.
Printed and bound in China.

A CIP catalogue for this book is available from the British Library

ISBN 978-0-85720-274-1

1 3 5 7 9 10 8 6 4 2

Pictured on the front cover: Roasted Vegetable Bagels p26, Garden Paella p84, Courgette Pots with Tomato Sauce p122, Baked Red Pepper Crumble p46.
Pictured on the introduction: Creamy Asparagus Pasta p54, Tofu and Vegetable Kebabs p96, Grilled Mediterranean Quiche p10, Broad Bean and Leek Tortilla p134.

ProPoints® value logo: You'll find this easy to read **ProPoints** value logo on every recipe throughout this book. The logo represents the number of **ProPoints** values per serving each recipe contains. It is not an indication of the fillingness of a recipe.

Weight Watchers **ProPoints** Weight Loss System is a simple way to lose weight. As part of the Weight Watchers **ProPoints** plan you'll enjoy eating delicious, healthy, filling foods that help to keep you feeling satisfied for longer and in control of your portions.

V This symbol denotes a vegetarian recipe and assumes that, where relevant, free range eggs, vegetarian cheese, vegetarian virtually fat free fromage frais, vegetarian low fat crème fraîche and vegetarian low fat yogurts are used. Virtually fat free fromage frais, low fat crème fraîche and low fat yogurts may contain traces of gelatine so they are not always vegetarian. Please check the labels.

* This symbol denotes a dish that can be frozen. Unless otherwise stated, you can freeze the finished dish for up to 3 months. Defrost thoroughly and reheat until the dish is piping hot throughout.

Recipe notes
Egg size: Medium, unless otherwise stated.
Raw eggs: Only the freshest eggs should be used. Pregnant women, the elderly and children should avoid recipes with eggs that are not fully cooked or raw.
All fruits and vegetables: Medium sized, unless otherwise stated.
Stock: Stock cubes used in recipes, unless otherwise stated. These should be prepared according to packet instructions.
Recipe timings: These are approximate and meant to be guidelines. Please note that the preparation time includes all the steps up to and following the main cooking time(s).
Microwaves: Timings and temperatures are for a standard 800 W microwave. If necessary, adjust to your own microwave.
Low fat spread: Where a recipe states to use a low fat spread, a light spread with a fat content of no less than 38% should be used.
Low fat soft cheese: Where low fat soft cheese is specified in a recipe, this refers to soft cheese with a fat content of less than 5%, such as Philadelphia Extra Light.

Contents

Introduction

Vegetarian food is exciting and delicious, and with *Cook Smart Vegetarian* you'll have plenty of inspiration. There is something here for every occasion, and dishes that are sure to appeal to everyone. So whether you are vegetarian or just wanting to try eating a little less meat, give these tasty recipes a try and surprise your family and friends.

About Weight Watchers

For more than 40 years Weight Watchers has been helping people around the world to lose weight using a long term sustainable approach. Weight Watchers successful weight loss system is based on four tried and trusted principles:

- Eating healthily
- Being more active
- Adjusting behaviour to help weight loss
- Getting support in weekly meetings

Our unique **ProPoints** system empowers you to manage your food plan and make wise recipe choices for a healthier, happier you.

Vegetarian Cooking

Vegetarian cooking is not just for people who don't eat meat, poultry or fish. Anyone can cook and enjoy vegetarian food, and you may find you enjoy these recipes so much you regularly swap your old favourite meat dishes for some new vegetarian ones. Many vegetarians eat eggs and dairy products, and in this book we have included recipes with these. If you are a vegetarian and following a more restrictive diet, please check the recipes to see whether they contain eggs or dairy products.

If you are going to cook healthy, nutritious meals, it is worth investing in some quality ingredients. Although this may be more expensive, the flavour will be better and you will enjoy your food far more, so buy the best you can afford. And if you enjoy what you eat, you are likely to cook more rather than reach for a takeaway menu.

Make the most of seasonal ingredients and don't be afraid of trying new vegetables and flavours. From vibrant winter cabbages to spring asparagus and from juicy summer fruit to autumnal squashes, seasonal fresh fruit and vegetables taste far better than frozen or canned. And by ringing the changes you'll be eating a greater variety of fruit and vegetables throughout the year. You'll be less likely to get bored with the same old meals and may even find new favourite ingredients.

Even changing staple foods like pasta and rice can increase flavour. Try imported dried pastas, which have a wheaty, bread-like taste and will stay al dente better than most other brands. Or swap plain white rice for basmati or jasmine rice and see the difference. Try some different varieties to find the one you like the most.

Worth Buying

It is worth keeping a few basics in your store cupboard that will add extra flavour to your dishes. This way you'll always have ingredients to create a tasty meal.

- Olive oil – a good quality extra virgin olive oil adds a wonderful flavour to salad dressings. Try a few brands to find one you like.

- Balsamic vinegar – balsamic vinegar is light and fruity. Buy the best you can find and try it drizzled over salads or vegetables.

- Porcini mushrooms – these mushrooms have an intense flavour but fresh ones are only available at certain times of the year. However dried porcini mushrooms are just as good and are available all year round. They are incredibly versatile and worth stocking for adding to stews, pasta and risottos.

- Parmesan cheese – if you are going to add a little cheese, it is worth making sure it is the best you can find. Avoid cheap but tasteless ready grated Parmesan and buy a block of Parmigiano-Reggiano instead. You can use a vegetable peeler to create shavings and the flavour will be well worth the extra expense.

- Honey – a drizzle of honey can make all the difference to a pancake or dessert. Specialist honey has flavour from the region in which it is produced, or from the flower or trees that the bees have predominantly visited. Try a few different types and you'll be amazed at the difference in flavour.

- Chocolate – a little also goes a long way with chocolate, but only if you use quality brands. Look for at least 70% cocoa solids – the stronger the chocolate taste, the less you will need.

Storing and Freezing

Once you have mastered the art of cooking delicious, healthy meals, you may want to make extra and store or freeze it for a later date. Store any leftovers in sealed containers in the fridge and use them up within a day or two. Many recipes can be frozen, as can individual ingredients, but it is important to make sure you know how to freeze safely.

- Wrap any food to be frozen in rigid containers or strong freezer bags. This is important to stop foods contaminating each other or getting freezer burn.

- Label the containers or bags with the contents and date – your freezer should have a star marking that tells you how long you can keep different types of frozen food.

- Never freeze warm food – always let it cool completely first.

- Never freeze food that has already been frozen and defrosted.

- Freeze food in portions, then you can take out as little or as much as you need each time.

- Defrost what you need in the fridge, making sure you put anything that might have juices on a covered plate or in a container.

Most fruit and vegetables can be frozen by open freezing. Lay them out on a tray and freeze until solid, then pack them into bags. Some vegetables, such as peas, broccoli and broad beans can be blanched first by cooking for 2 minutes in boiling water. Drain and refresh under cold water then freeze once cold. Fresh herbs are great frozen – either seal leaves in bags or, for soft herbs such as basil and parsley, chop finely and add to ice cube trays with water. These are great for dropping into casseroles or soups straight from the freezer.

Some things cannot be frozen. Whole eggs do not freeze well, but yolks and whites can be frozen separately. Vegetables with a high water content, such as salad leaves, celery and cucumber, will not freeze. Fried foods will be soggy if frozen, and sauces such as mayonnaise will separate when thawed and should not be frozen.

Lunches and Light Bites

From a leisurely lunch or light bite with a friend, to a sandwich to pop in your lunchbox, there are plenty of ideas here to keep you going. Try a Spanish Omelette, Halloumi Pitta, Caribbean Rice or Moroccan Stuffed Tomatoes.

Ring the changes for lunch
with these great ideas

Grilled Mediterranean Quiche

This quiche can be part prepared in advance, leaving you to just put it together and bake at the last minute for a special lunch with family or friends.

Serves 4

calorie controlled cooking spray
2 red peppers, de-seeded and cut into eighths
1 aubergine, cubed
2 courgettes, sliced lengthways into
  1 cm (½ inch) slices
2 small red onions, cut into wedges
2 tablespoons balsamic vinegar
a small bunch of fresh mint, chopped finely
1 garlic clove, crushed
2 eggs
150 ml (5 fl oz) skimmed milk
1 teaspoon French mustard
salt and freshly ground black pepper

For the pastry

50 g (1¾ oz) low fat spread
100 g (3½ oz) plain flour
a pinch of salt
1 egg white, beaten

---

5 **ProPoints** values per serving
20 **ProPoints** values per recipe

257 **calories** per serving

Takes **30 minutes** to prepare + **30 minutes** chilling, **1 hour 15 minutes** to cook

V

✳ not recommended

1 Preheat the oven to Gas Mark 7/220°C/fan oven 200°C. Spray a roasting tin with the cooking spray and put the vegetables in. Season, spray again with the cooking spray and sprinkle over the balsamic vinegar, mint and garlic. Roast for 30 minutes.

2 Meanwhile, make the pastry. Rub the low fat spread into the flour and a pinch of salt until it resembles fresh breadcrumbs. Add 1–2 tablespoons of water – just enough to bind it into a ball. Wrap in cling film and chill for 30 minutes.

3 Turn the oven down to Gas Mark 5/190°C/fan oven 170°C. Roll out the pastry and line a 19 cm (7½ inch) loose bottomed flan tin. Line with foil or baking parchment and fill with baking beans. Bake for 15 minutes then remove the beans and lining. Bake for a further 10 minutes.

4 Beat the eggs with the milk, seasoning and mustard. Spoon the cooked vegetables into the pastry case and pour over the egg mixture. Bake for 20 minutes until set and golden.

Spanish Omelette

This hearty omelette can be served warm straight from the pan, or it can be cooled for a packed lunch or picnic. Either way, it is great served with a crisp, zero *ProPoints* value green salad.

Serves 4

calorie controlled cooking spray
1 onion, sliced
1 red pepper, de-seeded and sliced
1 green pepper, de-seeded and sliced
125 ml (4 fl oz) vegetable stock
400 g (14 oz) potatoes, peeled and diced
6 eggs, beaten
salt and freshly ground black pepper

5 *ProPoints* values per serving
20 *ProPoints* values per recipe

239 calories per serving

Takes **25 minutes**

V

✳ not recommended

1 Heat a lidded non stick frying pan, spray with the cooking spray then stir fry the onion and peppers for 5 minutes until coloured. Add the stock, partially cover and simmer rapidly for 5 minutes until the vegetables are tender and the liquid has evaporated.

2 Meanwhile, bring a pan of water to the boil, add the potatoes and cook for 8–10 minutes until tender, then drain. Stir the potatoes into the frying pan with the peppers and onion.

3 Preheat the grill to a medium setting. Season the eggs then pour into the frying pan. Shake to settle the contents and cook over a gentle heat for 5 minutes until most of the egg has set.

4 Transfer to the grill, protecting the handle of the pan from the heat, and grill for 3 minutes to set the top. Cut into wedges and serve warm or cold.

Warm Goat's Cheese Salad

Although France is perhaps best known for its good quality goat's cheeses, there are some excellent ones from Wales and the West Country too. The flavours vary from very ripe and strong to mild and fresh, so you can experiment a bit with them.

Serves 4

175 g (6 oz) mixed salad leaves (such as rocket, frisée, oak-leaf, lamb's lettuce, radicchio), washed

a bunch of mixed fresh summer herbs (such as basil, chervil, coriander or parsley), washed

200 g (7 oz) baguette

100 g (3½ oz) goat's cheese with a crumbly/soft texture, such as a crottin

For the vinaigrette

1 tablespoon balsamic vinegar

2 teaspoons wholegrain mustard

2 tablespoons virtually fat free fromage frais

salt and freshly ground black pepper

6 *ProPoints* values per serving
25 *ProPoints* values per recipe

C **180 calories** per serving

Takes **15 minutes**

V

* not recommended

1 Put the salad leaves in a serving bowl with the herbs.

2 Heat the grill to high. Cut the bread into 20 diagonal slices to make large croûtons and spread each with a little goat's cheese. Place the croûtons under the grill for a few minutes or until beginning to brown at the edges.

3 Meanwhile, put all the vinaigrette ingredients into a screw top jar, screw on the lid and shake. Pour over the salad and toss together.

4 Place the croûtons on top of the salad and serve immediately.

Tip The fat content of goat's cheese does vary from cheese to cheese, so do check before you buy. Because the flavour is so pronounced, however, you only need to use a little to get a great taste.

Variation Try using 2 teaspoons of walnut or hazelnut oil instead of 2 tablespoons of fromage frais. These oils have a delicious nutty flavour that is excellent in this salad. The ***ProPoints*** values per serving will be 7.

Green Lentil Soup

This is a basic soup that can be varied in many ways by adding herbs or spices.

Serves 4

200 g (7 oz) dried green lentils
1 onion, chopped finely
1 garlic clove, crushed
1 litre (1¾ pints) vegetable stock
1 tablespoon cornflour
salt and freshly ground black pepper

5 **ProPoints** values per serving
20 **ProPoints** values per recipe

180 calories per serving

Takes **5 minutes** to prepare,
40 minutes to cook

V

* not recommended

1 Put the lentils, onion, garlic and stock in a large saucepan and bring to the boil.

2 Simmer for 40 minutes, until the lentils are soft.

3 Mix the cornflour with a little cold water and stir into the soup to thicken it slightly.

4 Season well and serve.

Variation Make this into green lentil and lemon soup by adding the juice of ½ a lemon before serving.

Halloumi Pitta

Sweet piquante peppers (Peppadew) are small, fairly hot peppers that are great to keep in the fridge.

Serves 1

70 g (2½ oz) halloumi light, sliced
1 wholemeal pitta bread
a handful of mixed salad leaves

For the salsa

1 sweet piquante pepper, i.e. Peppadew, cut into thin strips, plus 2 teaspoons juice from the jar
2 cm (¾ inch) cucumber, diced
1 teaspoon finely chopped red onion
1 tablespoon finely chopped coriander leaves

9 ProPoints values per serving
9 ProPoints values per recipe

340 calories per serving

Takes **10 minutes**

V

✳ not recommended

1 To make the salsa, place the pepper in a small bowl. Combine with the juice from the jar, cucumber, onion and coriander.

2 Preheat the grill to medium and line the grill pan with foil. Grill the halloumi slices for 3–4 minutes, until golden. At the same time, grill the pitta bread for 1 minute until warm.

3 Slit open the pitta bread and fill with the halloumi, salad leaves and salsa.

Tip Make a pot of this salsa to keep in the fridge for up to 3 days, only adding the coriander when required – it's great with grilled meats and fish or to jazz up a salad.

Cajun Potato Skins

This recipe uses a tasty salsa that is also delicious served with zero **ProPoints** value grilled vegetables.

Serves 4

3 x 225 g (8 oz) baking potatoes
2 teaspoons Cajun spice mix
1 tablespoon sunflower oil
1 teaspoon salt flakes

For the salsa

225 g (8 oz) mango, diced finely
1 red onion, chopped finely
finely grated zest and juice of a lime
1 teaspoon olive oil
225 g (8 oz) plum tomatoes, skinned and chopped finely
2 tablespoons chopped fresh coriander

1 Preheat the oven to Gas Mark 6/200°C/fan oven 180°C. Prick the potatoes all over and bake for 50 minutes. Carefully remove from the oven and slice in half.

2 Using a small spoon, scoop out the potato flesh from the centre of each half – don't discard the flesh as you can use it for mashed potato at a later date.

3 Cut each potato skin in half. Place the 12 potato skins in a large plastic container with a tight fitting lid and add the Cajun spice, oil and salt flakes. Shake the container well, so each potato skin gets a light coating.

4 Arrange the potato skins on a baking sheet lined with non stick baking parchment. Return them to the oven for 20 minutes, until they are crunchy.

5 To make the salsa, mix together all the salsa ingredients. Chill in the fridge until ready to serve. Serve three crispy Cajun skins per person with a bowl of salsa for dipping.

5 **ProPoints** values per serving
20 **ProPoints** values per recipe

225 **calories** per serving

Takes **20 minutes** to prepare + chilling,
1 hour 10 minutes to cook

V

* not recommended

Tips To speed things up you can microwave the potatoes, they will take roughly 5 minutes each on High.

Chick Pea Salad with Houmous Dressing

A lovely salad dish, this is ideal for a buffet if made in larger quantities. It is delicious accompanied by crusty bread but don't forget to add the extra *ProPoints* values.

Serves 2

a few lettuce leaves, torn into bite size leaves

8 cm (3¼ inches) cucumber, sliced

½ carrot, peeled and grated

440 g can chick peas, drained and rinsed

a few slices of red onion

2 tomatoes, cut into wedges

For the dressing

100 g (3½ oz) reduced fat houmous

4 teaspoons skimmed milk

1 Arrange the salad ingredients on two serving plates.

2 Whisk together the dressing ingredients and pour over the salads. Serve immediately.

8 *ProPoints* values per serving
15 *ProPoints* values per recipe

C **410 calories** per serving

⊙ Takes **5 minutes**

V

✱ not recommended

Curried Egg and Cress Pitta

For the perfect hard-boiled egg, place in a small pan of cold water, bring to the boil and simmer for 6–7 minutes. Cool under cold running water to prevent a dark ring from forming around the yolk.

Serves 1

1 wholemeal pitta bread
1 hard-boiled egg, peeled
2 tablespoons very low fat plain fromage frais
¼ teaspoon medium curry powder
2 tablespoons hot mustard cress, snipped
2 Little Gem lettuce leaves
salt and freshly ground black pepper

7 *ProPoints* values per serving
7 *ProPoints* values per recipe

C **252 calories** per serving

Takes **12 minutes**

V

✱ not recommended

1 Lightly toast the pitta bread under the grill or in a toaster.

2 Meanwhile, using a fork, mash the hard-boiled egg together with the fromage frais, curry powder and seasoning. Stir in the cress.

3 Split the pitta bread open and tuck the lettuce leaves inside the pocket. Spoon in the curried egg and cress filling and serve.

Pasta and Sweetcorn Salad

This recipe is just as easy to prepare as a sandwich – and very satisfying. It's also ideal for picnics and can very easily be multiplied to make extra servings.

Serves 1

40 g (1½ oz) dried pasta shells
50 g (1¾ oz) cherry tomatoes, halved
3 spring onions, chopped
5 cm (2 inch) cucumber, diced
2 tablespoons sweetcorn
1 celery stick, chopped finely
½ small orange or red pepper, de-seeded and diced
1 tablespoon low fat natural yogurt
1 tablespoon low fat mayonnaise
½ tablespoon chopped fresh parsley or chives
salt and freshly ground black pepper

To garnish
a little fresh parsley or chives, chopped
3 olives

---

8 *ProPoints* values per serving
8 *ProPoints* values per recipe

289 calories per serving

Takes **30 minutes**

V

✱ not recommended

1 Bring a pan of water to the boil, add the pasta and cook according to the packet instructions or until al dente. Drain, reserving ½ tablespoon of cooking water.

2 Put all the salad vegetables into a large salad bowl or lidded plastic box and mix the cooked pasta in.

3 Add the yogurt and mayonnaise to the reserved cooking water with some seasoning and mix together thoroughly – a mini whisk makes this very quick. Add the chopped herbs.

4 Stir the sauce straight into the salad and garnish with the herbs and olives. Serve immediately or transfer into a lunch box for later.

Variation This is a very flexible recipe – for variety, try adding a heaped tablespoon of kidney beans, for an extra 1 *ProPoints* value.

Broad Bean 'Guacamole'

This dish is derived from an ancient Arab recipe for 'bessara', a purée of broad beans and herbs. Serve with a lightly toasted medium pitta bread per person, adding 4 *ProPoints* values per serving.

Serves 2

300 g can broad beans, drained and rinsed

a small bunch of fresh coriander or parsley, chopped roughly

1 small green chilli, de-seeded and chopped finely (optional)

1 garlic clove, crushed

½ teaspoon ground cumin

1 small red onion, chopped roughly

juice of a lemon

salt and freshly ground black pepper

1 Place all the ingredients in a food processor and purée to a rough paste. Alternatively, crush the ingredients together with a pestle and mortar to achieve the same result. Check the seasoning and serve.

2 *ProPoints* values per serving
4 *ProPoints* values per recipe

75 calories per serving

Takes **5 minutes**

V

✱ not recommended

Aubergine Dip

This is a great zero *ProPoints* value dip – ideal for sharing with friends.

Serves 4

1 large aubergine
2 tablespoons lemon juice
grated zest of ¼ of a lemon
1 garlic clove
**2 tablespoons chopped fresh
  parsley or coriander**
½ teaspoon cumin seeds
**75 g (2¾ oz) 0% fat Greek
  yogurt**

**salt and freshly ground black
  pepper**

To serve

**1 red and 1 yellow pepper,
  2 carrots, 2 celery sticks and
  10 cm (4 inches) cucumber,
  all cut into sticks**

1 Preheat the oven to Gas Mark 6/200°C/fan oven 180°C. Put the aubergine on a baking sheet and bake for 40 minutes or until tender. Allow to cool.

2 Once cool, peel off the skin and put the flesh into a food processor along with all the remaining ingredients for the dip. Whizz until smooth. If you don't have a food processor, chop or mash the ingredients as finely as possible and crush the garlic clove. The dip may be a little chunkier but it will still taste great.

3 Transfer to a suitable container and chill for at least 2 hours. The flavour develops and changes in this time, so add seasoning if needed just before serving with the vegetable sticks.

0 *ProPoints* value per serving
1 *ProPoints* value per recipe

55 calories per serving

Takes **10 minutes** to prepare + cooling
+ chilling, **40 minutes to cook**

V

✱ not recommended

Roasted Vegetable Bagels

Make these delicious bagels to take to work – they are far tastier than shop-bought versions.

Serves 2

calorie controlled cooking spray
½ red pepper, de-seeded and sliced into 4 pieces
½ yellow or green pepper, de-seeded and sliced into 4 pieces
½ small courgette, sliced thinly
4 thin slices of aubergine (optional)
a few fresh basil leaves, torn into pieces
2 tablespoons balsamic vinegar
a dash of Tabasco sauce (optional)
2 plain bagels
75 g (2¾ oz) low fat soft cheese
salt and freshly ground black pepper

7 ProPoints values per serving
15 ProPoints values per recipe

280 calories per serving

Takes **15 minutes** to prepare + cooling, **5 minutes** to cook

V

✱ not recommended

1 Heat a griddle pan or non stick frying pan until hot, then spray with the cooking spray.

2 Put the peppers, courgette and aubergine (if using) into the pan. Cook for about 5 minutes, turning often until well done and pressing the vegetables down with a spatula to char them.

3 Tip the vegetables into a bowl and add the basil and balsamic vinegar. Season, add a dash of Tabasco sauce, if using, then mix well. Cover and leave to cool.

4 Slice the bagels in half and lightly toast the cut sides. Divide the soft cheese and spread evenly over both halves of each bagel. Arrange the vegetables over one half, sandwich together, then serve.

Tip You could soften the vegetables in the microwave for 2 minutes on High before roasting in the pan.

Variation Instead of low fat soft cheese, use 1 tablespoon of reduced fat houmous per bagel. The **ProPoints** values will remain the same.

Sweet and Sour Cauliflower Salad

U 3 ProPoints value

This is an unusual and tasty way to serve cauliflower. The sweet and sour dressing is delicious tossed with any crunchy zero **ProPoints** value vegetables.

Serves 2

1 small cauliflower
1 small red onion, sliced thinly
1 small courgette, cubed
½ yellow pepper, de-seeded and sliced finely
1 tablespoon chopped fresh parsley
salt and freshly ground black pepper

For the dressing

2 tablespoons light soy sauce
2 tablespoons white wine vinegar
1 tablespoon dry sherry (optional)
2 teaspoons clear honey
1 teaspoon sesame oil
4 tablespoons boiling water

1 Halve the cauliflower then remove the thick stalk and discard. Cut off the florets and trim their stalks right down. Bring a large saucepan of water to the boil, add the cauliflower florets, onion and courgette and blanch them for 2–3 minutes until they are tender, yet still crisp.

2 Drain the vegetables well and tip them into a large bowl. Whisk the dressing ingredients together and stir it into the cooling vegetables.

3 Add the pepper and parsley. Season and serve warm.

3 **ProPoints** values per serving
5 **ProPoints** values per recipe

C 95 calories per serving

Takes **20 minutes**

V

✳ not recommended

Cottage Cheese and Vermicelli Fritters

Quick and easy crispy fritters that are perfect for a snack.

Serves 4

175 g (6 oz) dried vermicelli
  noodles, broken up
3 eggs, separated
500 g (1 lb 2 oz) reduced fat
  plain cottage cheese
a bunch of spring onions,
  chopped finely

a packet of fresh chives,
  chopped
25 g (1 oz) plain flour
calorie controlled cooking spray
salt and freshly ground black
  pepper

1 Soak the noodles according to the packet instructions. Drain.

2 In a large bowl, mix the egg yolks with the noodles, cottage cheese, spring onions, chives, flour and seasoning. Whisk the egg whites until stiff and then fold into the cottage cheese mixture.

3 Preheat the oven to low. Spray a non stick frying pan with the cooking spray and place over a medium heat. Drop in spoonfuls of the mixture. Cook until the undersides are brown – about 6 minutes – and then turn with a fish slice and cook the other side. Place on a baking sheet lined with kitchen towel and keep warm in the oven until the others are cooked.

9 ProPoints values per serving
35 ProPoints values per recipe

C **365 calories** per serving

Takes **15 minutes** to prepare,
25 minutes to cook

V

✳ not recommended

Caribbean Rice

Full of flavour and colour, this is perfect for when you need something filling.

Serves 2

125 g (4½ oz) dried brown rice
75 g (2¾ oz) frozen peas
a kettleful of boiling water
½ red pepper, de-seeded and sliced finely
½ small red onion, diced finely
125 g (4½ oz) fresh or canned pineapple in natural juice, drained and cut into chunks
2 tablespoons chopped fresh coriander
1 tomato, de-seeded and diced finely
2 tablespoons Italian style fat free dressing
salt and freshly ground black pepper

7 ProPoints values per serving
15 ProPoints values per recipe

310 calories per serving

Takes **45 minutes**

V

✳ not recommended

1 Bring a large pan of water to the boil, add the rice, bring back to the boil and simmer for 30 minutes until tender. Drain and rinse in cold water until the rice is cold. Drain again thoroughly.

2 Meanwhile, put the frozen peas into a bowl and pour over the boiling water. Leave for 5 minutes. Drain and put into a large bowl.

3 Add the rice to the peas along with the pepper, onion, pineapple, coriander and tomato. Stir though the Italian dressing, season to taste and serve.

Moroccan Stuffed Tomatoes

A filling lunch dish that combines couscous with the sweet and tangy, hot and minty flavours of North African cuisine.

Serves 4

8 beefsteak tomatoes
150 g (5½ oz) dried couscous
½ a kettleful of boiling water
2 teaspoons cumin seeds
calorie controlled cooking spray
2 garlic cloves, crushed
25 g (1 oz) dried apricots, chopped finely
100 g (3½ oz) Feta cheese
1 teaspoon Tabasco sauce
a small bunch of fresh mint leaves, chopped
grated zest and juice of a lemon
a small bunch of fresh parsley, chopped finely
salt and freshly ground black pepper

6 *ProPoints* values per serving
23 *ProPoints* values per recipe

C   **250 calories** per serving

Takes **15 minutes** to prepare,
20 minutes to cook

V

✻   not recommended

1 Preheat the oven to Gas Mark 7/220°C/fan oven 200°C. Slice the tops off the tomatoes and carefully scoop out the flesh to leave a sturdy shell. Chop and reserve the flesh. Place the tomato shells on a baking sheet.

2 Place the couscous in a bowl and pour over enough boiling water to cover. Place a plate over the top and leave to steam for 5 minutes.

3 Meanwhile, heat a non stick frying pan and dry fry the cumin seeds until they pop and become fragrant. Put aside and spray the pan with the cooking spray. Stir fry the garlic for a few minutes, until golden.

4 Add the toasted cumin seeds, garlic and all the remaining ingredients, including the chopped tomato flesh to the couscous. Mix well and then spoon the mixture into the tomato shells. Bake for 20 minutes, until golden and heated through.

Creamy Celery Soup

Celeriac not only adds flavour to this soup, it also thickens it and makes it creamy.

Serves 2

calorie controlled cooking spray
1 onion, sliced
2 celery sticks, chopped, leaves reserved
200 g (7 oz) celeriac, peeled and diced
1 bay leaf
600 ml (20 fl oz) vegetable stock

1 *ProPoints* value per serving
2 *ProPoints* values per recipe

56 calories per serving

Takes **10 minutes** to prepare,
20 minutes to cook

V

✳ recommended

1 Lightly spray a large, lidded, non stick pan with the cooking spray and heat until hot. Add the vegetables and stir fry for 3–4 minutes until beginning to soften.

2 Add the bay leaf and stock. Bring to the boil, cover and simmer for 20 minutes until the vegetables are soft. Remove from the heat, take out the bay leaf and blend until smooth, either with a hand held blender or transfer to a liquidiser.

3 Gently reheat the soup to warm it through. Serve garnished with the reserved celery leaves.

Variation Celeriac is a winter root vegetable with a hard texture like parsnip but with the flavour of celery. If you can't find it, use the equivalent weight in peeled and chopped potatoes, adding an extra celery stick, for 3 *ProPoints* values per serving.

Falafels with Moroccan Orange Salad

6 ProPoints value

Serves 6

250 g (9 oz) dried chick peas
400 g can chick peas, drained, reserving
  2 tablespoons of liquid
1 small garlic clove
1 tablespoon tahini
4 spring onions, chopped finely
a small bunch of fresh coriander, chopped
1 teaspoon ground coriander
1 teaspoon ground cumin
¼ teaspoon dried chilli flakes, or more to taste
juice of a lemon
calorie controlled cooking spray
salt and freshly ground black pepper

For the salad

4 carrots, peeled and grated coarsely
200 g (7 oz) cabbage, shredded finely
2 oranges, peeled and cut into segments,
  reserving any juice
juice of an orange
25 g (1 oz) flaked almonds, toasted

 6 ProPoints values per serving
38 ProPoints values per recipe

C **294 calories** per serving

Takes **30 minutes** to prepare + soaking,
40–45 minutes to bake

V

✻ recommended after step 2

1 Place the dried chick peas in a bowl, cover with plenty of water and leave to soak for at least 2 hours or overnight.

2 Preheat the oven to Gas Mark 4/180°C/fan oven 160°C. Drain the soaked chick peas, rinse thoroughly and place in a food processor. Whizz to a paste-like consistency, stopping to scrape the sides and stir the mixture.

3 Add the other ingredients, apart from the salad and the cooking spray, including the 2 tablespoons of liquid from the can of chick peas. Whizz, stopping and stirring occasionally, until the mixture holds together when you roll it. Using your hands, make 30 walnut size balls.

4 Spray a non stick baking tray with the cooking spray and place the falafels on the tray. Bake for 40–45 minutes until golden.

5 Meanwhile, make the salad by gently tossing all the ingredients together with seasoning. Serve with the falafels.

Spinach and Feta Pastries

These tasty Greek pastries are delicious eaten on their own for a snack or a packed lunch, or serve them with a zero **ProPoints** value salad or zero **ProPoints** value vegetables for a more substantial meal.

Serves 6

750 g (1 lb 10 oz) fresh spinach leaves, washed thoroughly
calorie controlled cooking spray
1 onion, chopped finely
1 garlic clove, crushed
2 teaspoons Italian mixed dried herbs
1 egg, beaten
6 x 15 g filo pastry sheets, measuring 30 x 17 cm (12 x 7 inches), defrosted if frozen
100 g (3½ oz) Feta cheese, crumbled
salt and freshly ground black pepper

---

2 ProPoints values per serving
15 ProPoints values per recipe

165 calories per serving

Takes **20 minutes** to prepare + cooling, **30–35 minutes** to cook

V

✱ recommended

1 Preheat the oven to Gas Mark 6/200°C/fan oven 180°C.

2 Pack the spinach into a large saucepan and cook, without adding any water, for 3–4 minutes until the leaves have wilted. Drain well, squeezing out any excess moisture with the back of a spoon. Cool and chop roughly.

3 Heat a non stick frying pan and spray with the cooking spray. Add the onion and garlic and sauté gently for 3–4 minutes, until softened. Remove from the heat, allow to cool and then mix in the herbs, egg and spinach. Season.

4 Lightly spray a non stick baking sheet or Swiss roll tin with the cooking spray. Lay one filo pastry sheet on top and lightly spray it with the cooking spray. If the pastry sheet is too big, just fold in the edges. Repeat the process with two more filo pastry sheets. Spoon on the filling, spreading it out evenly, and then sprinkle the Feta cheese over the top.

5 Lay the remaining pastry sheets over the filling, spraying them with the cooking spray as before, and then spray the surface.

6 Bake for 30–35 minutes, until the pastry is golden. Cool for a few minutes and then cut into six portions.

Tip Keep filo pastry covered with cling film or a damp tea towel as you work to prevent it drying out.

Button Mushroom Provençal

7 ProPoints value

Serve this as a tasty snack or light lunch with a mixed zero *ProPoints* value green salad.

Serves 2

1 teaspoon olive oil
350 g (12 oz) button mushrooms
2 shallots, chopped finely
1 garlic clove, crushed
4 tablespoons medium white wine
225 g can chopped tomatoes
½ teaspoon caster sugar
2 x 75 g (2¾ oz) slices French bread
2 tablespoons chopped fresh parsley
salt and freshly ground black pepper

1 Heat the oil in a frying pan and add the mushrooms, shallots and garlic. Stir fry for 2 minutes and then add the wine, tomatoes and sugar.

2 Bring to the boil and cook over a fairly high heat for 10 minutes until the sauce reduces a little.

3 Meanwhile, toast the French bread slices until they are lightly golden. It may be easiest to do this under the grill.

4 Once the mushroom sauce has reduced, stir in the parsley and season to taste.

5 Arrange the toasts on two serving plates and spoon the mushrooms on top.

7 *ProPoints* values per serving
14 *ProPoints* values per recipe

C **395 calories** per serving

Takes **10 minutes** to prepare,
15 minutes to cook

V

✳ not recommended

Tips For the best results, chose firm small mushrooms. Any large mushrooms should be halved.

For a more interesting version of this dish, try using a selection of mushrooms, such as chestnut, shiitake, oyster or any of the wild mushrooms that are available in the supermarkets. The *ProPoints* values will be the same.

Thai Sweetcorn Fritters with Salsa

A great snack for a summer lunch – delicately flavoured sweetcorn fritters with a spicy, refreshing salsa.

Serves 2

60 g (2 oz) plain flour
a pinch of chilli powder
a pinch of salt
1 small egg, beaten
80 ml (2¾ fl oz) reduced fat
  coconut milk
125 g (4½ oz) canned sweetcorn,
  drained

2 spring onions, sliced
calorie controlled cooking spray

For the salsa
½ red onion, diced
¼ cucumber, diced
2 tomatoes, diced
1 tablespoon rice vinegar

1 Sift the flour, chilli powder and salt into a bowl and make a well in the centre. Add the beaten egg and coconut milk and beat to make a smooth batter. Add the sweetcorn and spring onions and mix well.

2 Spray a non stick frying pan with the cooking spray and heat. Place individual tablespoonfuls of the sweetcorn batter into the pan and cook for 5–6 minutes. Then turn over and cook on the other side for 4–5 minutes, until golden. Remove from the pan and keep warm whilst cooking the remaining batter in the same way. The batter allows for 6 small or 4 medium fritters.

3 Mix the salsa ingredients together and serve with the sweetcorn fritters.

7 ProPoints values per serving
14 ProPoints values per recipe

C **265 calories** per serving

Takes **10 minutes** to prepare,
20 minutes to cook

V

* not recommended

Tip Vinegars are widely used in Eastern cooking and, unlike Western vinegars, they are usually made from rice. If you cannot get rice vinegar substitute cider vinegar. The **ProPoints** values will remain the same.

Roasted Pepper Couscous Salad

6 ProPoints value

Perfect for a packed lunch, this flavoursome and colourful couscous salad makes a great change from everyday sandwiches.

Serves 1

50 g (1¾ oz) dried couscous
75 ml (3 fl oz) boiling water
60 g (2 oz) broccoli, cut into small florets
1 roasted red pepper in brine from a jar, drained and sliced
8 cherry tomatoes, halved
1 tablespoon fresh basil, shredded
25 g (1 oz) light Feta cheese, crumbled
salt and freshly ground black pepper

6 *ProPoints* values per serving
6 *ProPoints* values per recipe

C **285 calories** per serving

Takes **8 minutes**

V

＊ not recommended

1 Place the couscous in a bowl and pour over the boiling water. Stir, cover with a plate and leave to stand for 5 minutes to absorb the liquid and soften. Fluff up with a fork when ready.

2 Meanwhile, bring a pan of water to the boil, add the broccoli and cook for 3 minutes. Drain, rinse with cold water and drain again.

3 Mix the broccoli into the couscous, followed by the roasted pepper, tomatoes, basil and Feta cheese. Season and tip into a lidded plastic box. Chill until ready to serve.

Tip For a no-cook salad, replace the broccoli with diced raw courgette, cucumber or radishes. The *ProPoints* values will remain the same.

Warm Broccoli Salad with Mustard Dressing

A light lunch or supper dish with satisfyingly strong flavours. For an al fresco lunch, try serving it with 150 g (5½ oz) minted new potatoes per person, for an extra 3 **ProPoints** values per serving.

Serves 2

1 small head of broccoli, cut into bite size pieces
1 small cauliflower, cut into bite size pieces

For the dressing
1 tablespoon Dijon mustard
4 tablespoons low fat natural yogurt
a small bunch of fresh parsley
salt and freshly ground black pepper

1 **ProPoints** value per serving
3 **ProPoints** values per recipe

C **170 calories** per serving

Takes **10 minutes**

V

* not recommended

1 Bring a large pan of water to the boil, add the broccoli and cauliflower and simmer for 4–5 minutes, until just tender.

2 Meanwhile, place all the dressing ingredients together in a bowl and stir together. Drain the vegetables and return to the pan. Pour over the dressing and toss together. Serve.

Herby Drop Scones with Chargrilled Vegetables

As children, many of us loved Scotch pancakes, fresh from the griddle, in time for tea. Times have moved on and now you can enjoy a modern, savoury version with a continental twist.

Serves 4

100 g (3½ oz) self raising flour

4 tablespoons chopped fresh herbs e.g. chives, oregano, basil (or 1 teaspoon dried)

1 egg, beaten

150 ml (5 fl oz) skimmed milk

1 yellow pepper, de-seeded and sliced into rings

2 courgettes, sliced diagonally

calorie controlled cooking spray

2 large tomatoes, sliced thickly

100 g (3½ oz) reduced fat mozzarella cheese, sliced

salt and freshly ground black pepper

8 fresh basil leaves, to garnish

4 *ProPoints* values per serving
17 *ProPoints* values per recipe

215 calories per serving

Takes **25 minutes**

V

* not recommended

1 Place the flour, herbs, egg, milk and seasoning in a liquidiser or food processor and blend to a stiff batter. Leave to stand while you cook the vegetables.

2 Heat a non stick frying pan and dry fry the pepper and courgettes until just softened and turning golden. Remove from the pan. Preheat the grill to medium.

3 Lightly spray the frying pan with the cooking spray. Add the batter in large tablespoons and cook until bubbles appear on the surface. Flip over the scones and cook the other side until golden. Keep warm in a clean tea towel while you cook the remaining batch, to make 8 scones in total.

4 Place a couple of slices of courgette, a ring of pepper, a tomato slice and a mozzarella slice on each scone. Grill until the cheese is melted and golden. Season well with black pepper. Serve, topped with a fresh basil leaf.

Weekday Suppers

When time is at a premium, give these recipes a go. From Stuffed Field Mushrooms to Butternut Squash and Boursin Risotto, Baked Leek and Mustard Gratin and Creamy Red Pepper Spaghetti, all can be prepared and cooked in an hour or less.

Weekday meals needn't mean reaching for the takeaway menu

Baked Red Pepper Crumble

Serve this delicious pasta dish with a zero *ProPoints* value fresh green salad.

Serves 4

400 g (14 oz) fresh penne pasta
700 g jar passata with onion and garlic
12 black olives in brine, drained
4 spring onions, sliced finely
10 fresh basil leaves, torn
200 g (7 oz) roasted red peppers in brine,
  drained and sliced finely
75 g (2¾ oz) dolcelatte cheese, crumbled
30 g (1¼ oz) Parmesan cheese, grated
½ medium slice white bread, diced finely
calorie controlled cooking spray
salt and freshly ground black pepper

11 *ProPoints* values per serving
44 *ProPoints* values per recipe

C **325 calories** per serving

Takes **20 minutes** to prepare,
25 minutes to cook

V

✱ not recommended

1 Preheat the oven to Gas Mark 4/180°C/fan oven 160°C. Bring a large pan of water to the boil and blanch the penne for 1 minute. Drain, reserving 100 ml (3½ fl oz) of cooking water and return both the penne and reserved liquid to the pan.

2 Stir in the passata, olives, spring onions and basil leaves. Season. Spoon into a 1 litre (1¾ pint) ovenproof dish. Scatter over the peppers and dolcelatte cheese and top with 1 tablespoon of the Parmesan cheese and the bread.

3 Spray with the cooking spray and bake in the oven for 25 minutes until golden and the pasta is cooked. Sprinkle with the remaining Parmesan cheese and serve.

Noodle Pancakes with Black Bean Quorn

Savoury black bean sauce is delicious with crunchy mixed peppers. Noodle and spring onion pancakes complete the meal.

Serves 4

125 g (4½ oz) dried medium egg noodles
50 g (1¾ oz) plain flour
1 egg
2 tablespoons skimmed milk
a bunch of spring onions, chopped roughly
calorie controlled cooking spray
350 g packet Quorn Chicken Style Pieces
3 mixed peppers, de-seeded and chopped roughly
195 g jar black bean sauce
salt and freshly ground black pepper

9 *ProPoints* values per serving
36 *ProPoints* values per recipe

C **333 calories** per serving

Takes **20 minutes**

V

✳ not recommended

1 Bring a pan of water to the boil, add the noodles and cook for 4 minutes. Meanwhile, in a bowl, whisk the flour, egg and milk together with seasoning to make a thick batter. Drain the noodles, rinse in cold water, then snip into short lengths using scissors and stir into the batter with half the spring onions.

2 Heat a non stick frying pan and spray with the cooking spray. Spoon half the noodle mixture into the pan as four separate pancakes and fry for 2½ minutes on each side over a high heat. Keep warm while you use the remaining mixture to make another four pancakes.

3 Meanwhile, spray a separate non stick frying pan or wok with the cooking spray. Stir fry the Quorn and peppers for 5 minutes. Add the remaining spring onions to the pan, followed by the black bean sauce and 150 ml (5 fl oz) of water. Simmer for 5 minutes, then serve two pancakes each with the Quorn mixture spooned over.

Mushroom Stroganoff

This creamy, filling stroganoff can be made hotter if you wish just by adding slightly more paprika. Serve with freshly cooked runner beans, for no additional **ProPoints** values.

Serves 4

calorie controlled cooking spray
1 large onion, chopped
450 g (1 lb) chestnut mushrooms, quartered
2 teaspoons paprika
400 g can chopped tomatoes
2 tablespoons half fat crème fraîche
salt and freshly ground black pepper

1 **ProPoints** value per serving
4 **ProPoints** values per recipe

C 65 calories per serving

Takes **10 minutes** to prepare,
25 minutes to cook

V

✻ recommended for up to **1 month**

1 Spray a medium lidded saucepan with the cooking spray and add the onion. Cover and leave to sweat on a low heat for 4–6 minutes, until the onion starts to soften.

2 Add the mushrooms and stir in the paprika. Cook for 1–2 minutes.

3 Pour in the tomatoes with 150 ml (5 fl oz) of water. Bring the mixture to a simmer and continue to simmer for 15 minutes.

4 Remove the pan from the heat and stir in the crème fraîche. Season to taste. Serve on four warmed plates.

Variations Shiitake or oyster mushrooms also work well in this recipe.

Try serving this dish with 40 g (1½ oz) of dried rice per person, cooked according to packet instructions, to soak up all the lovely sauce. This will add an extra 4 **ProPoints** values per serving.

Spinach, Egg and Cheese Ramekins

4 ProPoints value

Balance heartier winter dishes with this light savoury supper.

Serves 4

4 eggs
675 g (1½ lb) spinach, washed
50 g (1¾ oz) mature Cheddar cheese, grated
salt and freshly ground black pepper

For the sauce

400 g can chopped tomatoes
1 tablespoon finely chopped onion
½ teaspoon dried oregano or basil
½ teaspoon sugar
3 tablespoons virtually fat free fromage frais
salt and freshly ground black pepper

*4 **ProPoints** values per serving*
*15 **ProPoints** values per recipe*

210 calories per serving

Takes **20 minutes**

V

✻ not recommended

1 To make the sauce, place the tomatoes, onion, oregano or basil, and sugar in a small pan and bring to the boil, then simmer for 10 minutes. Season to taste. Blend the sauce to a purée in a liquidiser or food processor, then beat in the fromage frais. Preheat the grill.

2 Meanwhile, bring a pan of water to the boil, add the eggs and boil for 4 minutes. Remove from the water, shell and keep them in a bowl of warm water.

3 Cook the spinach in a small amount of boiling water for 3–4 minutes or until tender. Drain well and chop. Divide between four 10 cm (4 inch) ramekins, making a dip in the centre of each. Place an egg in each 'nest'.

4 Spoon the warmed sauce over the eggs. Sprinkle on the cheese and place under the grill for 3–4 minutes until the cheese has melted and is bubbling. Serve immediately.

Butternut Squash and Boursin Risotto

Risottos are at their best when served immediately, when the texture of the rice is just creamy. When left to cool, the rice becomes stodgy.

Serves 4

1 tablespoon olive oil
4 shallots, chopped
350 g (12 oz) butternut squash, peeled, de-seeded and diced
225 g (8 oz) dried risotto rice
150 ml (5 fl oz) white wine
600 ml (20 fl oz) vegetable stock
100 g (3½ oz) low fat Boursin with garlic and herbs
salt and freshly ground black pepper

8 ProPoints values per serving
33 ProPoints values per recipe

360 calories per serving

Takes **15 minutes** to prepare,
25 minutes to cook

V

✱ not recommended

1 Heat the oil in a large non stick pan and cook the shallots until softened. Add the squash and rice and cook for a further 2 minutes.

2 Gradually add the wine and stock, a little at a time, and cook, stirring, until the rice has absorbed all the stock, the squash is tender and the risotto has a creamy texture. This should take about 20 minutes. Season to taste and then stir in the Boursin.

3 Continue stirring until the Boursin has melted and serve at once.

Variation Diced pumpkin or courgette could be used instead of butternut squash if preferred. A little grated orange or lemon zest is also nice. The **ProPoints** values will remain the same.

Creamy Asparagus Pasta

This simple sauce does not detract from the fabulous flavour of asparagus.

Serves 4

350 g (12 oz) dried ribbon pasta

450 g (1 lb) asparagus, woody bases removed,
  cut into 2.5 cm (1 inch) lengths

2 tablespoons low fat fromage frais

grated zest and juice of a lemon

calorie controlled cooking spray

30 g (1¼ oz) fresh breadcrumbs

salt and freshly ground black pepper

9 *ProPoints* values per serving
37 *ProPoints* values per recipe

370 calories per serving

Takes **5 minutes** to prepare,
10 minutes to cook

V

* not recommended

1 Bring a pan of water to the boil, add the pasta and cook according to the packet instructions or until al dente.

2 Meanwhile, steam the asparagus or cook it in an inch of boiling water for 4 minutes in a lidded pan, until tender.

3 Preheat the grill to medium. Drain the pasta and mix with the asparagus, fromage frais, lemon juice and seasoning.

4 Spray a baking tray with the cooking spray, scatter over the breadcrumbs, spray again and toast under a medium grill until golden brown.

5 Mix the toasted breadcrumbs with the lemon zest and sprinkle over the top of the pasta before serving.

Mixed Vegetable Sushi

Now that the ingredients are widely available in the Oriental sections of supermarkets as well as Oriental food stores, it is surprisingly easy to make your own sushi... and it doesn't have to include raw fish.

Serves 4

225 g (8 oz) dried sushi rice
3 tablespoons seasoned rice vinegar or sherry
140 g (5 oz) mixed vegetables, cut into matchsticks (e.g. carrots, cucumber, baby corn, cooked beetroot)
calorie controlled cooking spray
2 eggs, lightly beaten
8 sheets nori

To serve

½ teaspoon wasabi paste
½ teaspoon pickled ginger
1 tablespoon soy sauce

7 *ProPoints* values per serving
27 *ProPoints* values per recipe

C **280 calories** per serving

Takes **30 minutes** to prepare, **20 minutes** to cook

V

✱ not recommended

1 Bring a pan of water to the boil, add the rice and cook according to the packet instructions. Stir in the vinegar or sherry and set aside.

2 Meanwhile, bring another pan of water to the boil and blanch the carrot sticks and baby corn for 2–3 minutes.

3 Heat a small omelette or non stick frying pan and spray with the the cooking spray, then pour in the beaten eggs and swirl around so that they cover the pan base. Cook until just set, then tip out and allow to cool. Cut into strips the same size as the vegetables.

4 Lay one sheet of the nori on a board and trim off the top third. Spread about 50 g (1¾ oz) of the rice along the front end, flatten slightly then place a strip of omelette and strips of vegetables on top.

5 Roll up tightly to form a log and stick the nori to itself by dampening with a brush dipped in water. Cut into 5–6 thick slices.

6 Repeat with the remaining rice, omelette and vegetable strips to make a selection of different fillings. Arrange on individual serving plates and serve each with a little pile of wasabi, pickled ginger and a dish of soy sauce for dipping.

Tuscan Beans

Delicious served on its own or with a crunchy salad of mixed leaves, vine ripened tomatoes and thin slices of red onion tossed with a drizzle of balsamic vinegar and seasoning, for no extra **ProPoints** values.

Serves 2

calorie controlled cooking spray
1 small onion, chopped finely
1 garlic clove, crushed
½ red pepper, de-seeded and chopped finely
100 g (3½ oz) mushrooms, chopped finely
1 courgette, diced finely
a small bunch of fresh rosemary, woody stems removed, tender stems and leaves chopped
150 g (5½ oz) passata
400 g can pinto beans, drained and rinsed
salt and freshly ground black pepper
a small bunch of fresh flat leaf parsley, chopped, to garnish (optional)

4 ProPoints values per serving
8 ProPoints values per recipe

200 calories per serving

Takes **20 minutes**

V

✳ recommended

1 Heat a large non stick saucepan and spray with the cooking spray. Fry the onion and garlic for 5 minutes with a few tablespoons of water, until softened.

2 Add the pepper, mushrooms and courgette and stir fry again for a few minutes then add the rosemary and passata.

3 Stir together and then add the beans and seasoning to the pan. Simmer for 5 minutes and serve scattered with the parsley, if using.

Creamy Red Pepper Spaghetti

This creamy, cheesy sauce tastes really luxurious. The roasted peppers have a lovely sweet flavour, which is really brought to life in this dish.

Serves 2

175 g (6 oz) dried wholemeal quick cook spaghetti
2 courgettes, sliced into rounds
calorie controlled cooking spray
2 roasted red peppers in brine, drained and sliced
60 g (2 oz) low fat soft cheese with garlic and herbs
1 tablespoon grated Parmesan cheese
freshly ground black pepper
2 tablespoons fresh basil leaves, to garnish

---

10 *ProPoints* values per serving
20 *ProPoints* values per recipe

C **380 calories** per serving

🕑 Takes **20 minutes**

V

✳ not recommended

1 Bring a large pan of water to the boil, add the spaghetti and cook for 10–12 minutes or until al dente.

2 Meanwhile, preheat the grill. Lightly spray the courgettes with the cooking spray and then grill for 2–3 minutes on each side until browned.

3 Drain the pasta, reserving 2 tablespoons of the cooking water. Place three quarters of the sliced peppers in a blender with the soft cheese and the 2 tablespoons of cooking water. Blend to a smooth sauce.

4 Pour the pepper sauce into a pan, add the remaining sliced peppers and heat through gently. Mix the pasta and Parmesan into the sauce and season with black pepper.

5 Divide the spaghetti and sauce between two warmed bowls, then scatter the courgettes on top and garnish with basil leaves. Serve immediately.

Spinach Scotch Pancakes

A great quick supper or brunch dish.

Serves 2

110 g (4 oz) self raising flour
1 egg
100 ml (3½ fl oz) skimmed milk
110 g (4 oz) frozen chopped spinach, defrosted,
  drained and excess water squeezed out
calorie controlled cooking spray
4 Quorn Deli Bacon Style Rashers
2 eggs
salt and freshly ground black pepper

---

10 *ProPoints* values per serving
20 *ProPoints* values per recipe

C 426 calories per serving

Takes 20 minutes

V

* recommended (pancakes only)

1 Place the flour in a large bowl, make a well in the centre and add the egg. Use a wooden spoon to mix carefully, drawing in the flour. Gradually add the milk to make a thick smooth batter. Stir in the spinach and season.

2 Lightly spray a non stick frying pan with the cooking spray and heat until hot. Place spoonfuls of the mixture in the pan (you should have enough to make four pancakes), leaving room for them to spread. Cook for 1–2 minutes until beginning to brown underneath, then turn and cook for a further 1–2 minutes. Set aside and keep warm.

3 Spray the pan again and cook the Quorn rashers for 1 minute on each side until golden.

4 Meanwhile, bring a large shallow pan of water to the boil and let it simmer. Crack 1 egg into a ramekin. Swirl the simmering water in the pan and, while doing so, carefully add the egg to the pan. This will bring the egg white into a rounded shape. Repeat with the second egg. Cook the eggs for 3 minutes then remove with a slotted spoon.

5 Serve two pancakes each, topped with a poached egg and two Quorn rashers.

Sicilian Aubergine Stew with Polenta

A filling supper dish. Look for instant dried polenta to save time.

Serves 4

calorie controlled cooking spray
1 large onion, chopped
2 garlic cloves, chopped
4 celery sticks, chopped
2 aubergines, cubed
400 g can chopped tomatoes
2 tablespoons tomato purée
3 tablespoons red wine vinegar
2 teaspoons caster sugar
2 tablespoons raisins
2 tablespoons capers in brine
20 black or green olives in brine, stoned and
  sliced
25 g (1 oz) pine nut kernels
400 g (14 oz) dried polenta
300 ml (10 fl oz) vegetable stock
salt and freshly ground black pepper
a small bunch of fresh parsley, chopped, to garnish

13 ProPoints values per serving
50 ProPoints values per recipe

498 calories per serving

Takes **25 minutes** to prepare,
20 minutes to cook

V

✱ recommended

1 Heat a large, lidded, non stick saucepan and spray with the cooking spray. Add the onion and garlic and cook for 2–3 minutes, until softened, adding a little water if necessary to prevent them from sticking.

2 Add the celery, aubergines, tomatoes, tomato purée, red wine vinegar, sugar, raisins, capers, olives and seasoning and bring to the boil.

3 Simmer, covered, for 20 minutes, stirring frequently, and then stir in the pine nut kernels.

4 Meanwhile, make up the polenta with the stock as directed on the packet.

5 Serve the stew with the polenta, scattered with the chopped parsley.

Baked Leek and Mustard Gratin

Serve this dish with a 225 g (8 oz) potato per person, baked in its skin, for 5 additional *ProPoints* values per serving.

Serves 4

700 g (1 lb 9 oz) baby leeks, cut in half lengthways then into long pieces and washed

50 g (1¾ oz) low fat spread

50 g (1¾ oz) plain flour

600 ml (20 fl oz) skimmed milk

1 bay leaf

100 g (3½ oz) low fat soft cheese with garlic and herbs

1 tablespoon wholegrain Dijon mustard

50 g (1¾ oz) half fat Cheddar cheese

salt and freshly ground black pepper

---

6 *ProPoints* values per serving
22 *ProPoints* values per recipe

247 calories per serving

Takes **10 minutes** to prepare,
50 minutes to cook

V

* recommended

1 Preheat the oven to Gas Mark 5/190°C/fan oven 170°C. Steam or boil the leeks for 5–10 minutes or until softened.

2 Meanwhile, melt the low fat spread in a non stick saucepan and stir in the flour to make a roux ball. Remove the pan from the heat, add the milk and bay leaf and whisk until the roux ball is completely broken up into the milk and you have a smooth sauce.

3 Return to a low heat and whisk until the sauce thickens. Add the soft cheese and mustard and season to taste.

4 Place the steamed leeks in the base of an ovenproof dish. Pour over the sauce and sprinkle with the cheese, then bake for 15 minutes until bubbling and golden.

Creamy Mushroom Tagliatelle

The perfect recipe for those busy days when you want to spend as little time as possible in the kitchen.

Serves 4

15 g (½ oz) dried porcini mushrooms
¼ kettleful of boiling water
250 g (9 oz) dried tagliatelle
calorie controlled cooking spray
225 g (8 oz) fresh chestnut mushrooms, sliced
1 garlic clove, crushed (optional)
400 g (14 oz) low fat soft cheese
1 tablespoon chopped fresh tarragon, plus extra
    sprigs to garnish (optional)
salt and freshly ground black pepper

---

9 *ProPoints* values per serving
37 *ProPoints* values per recipe

C **432 calories** per serving

Takes **15 minutes** + soaking

V

✴ not recommended

1 Put the porcini mushrooms in a small heatproof jug or bowl. Pour over enough boiling water to cover and leave to soak for at least 20 minutes, then drain. Chop any particularly large pieces into smaller chunks.

2 While the mushrooms are soaking, bring a large pan of water to the boil, add the tagliatelle and cook for 12 minutes or according to the packet instructions.

3 Meanwhile, heat a large non stick saucepan and spray it with the cooking spray. Cook the fresh mushrooms for 5 minutes until softened but not browned. Towards the end of the cooking time, stir in the garlic, if using.

4 Reduce the heat and add the soft cheese, porcini mushrooms and tarragon. Stir gently until the cheese has melted into a thick sauce. Season to taste.

5 Warm four bowls. Drain the pasta, reserving at least 100 ml (3½ fl oz) of the cooking water. Add the pasta to the cheese sauce and stir well. Add 4 tablespoons of the cooking liquid, stir in well and check the seasoning. If the pasta has soaked up a lot of the sauce and looks a little dry, add a little more cooking liquid. Serve immediately in the warmed bowls, garnished with more tarragon, if using.

Tip Always take the drained pasta to the pan with the sauce in it and add pasta to sauce, rather than the other way around. It really does make it easier to achieve a good coating of sauce on the pasta.

Nutty Chick Pea Crumble

8 ProPoints value

A very substantial meal, to be enjoyed by all.

Serves 6

calorie controlled cooking spray
1 onion, chopped
2 garlic cloves, crushed
1 celery stick, sliced
2 carrots, peeled and chopped
4 tomatoes, chopped
125 g (4½ oz) baby corn, halved
50 g (1¾ oz) dried red lentils
410 g can chick peas
300 ml (10 fl oz) vegetable stock
salt and freshly ground black pepper

For the crumble

50 g (1¾ oz) cashew nuts
60 g (2 oz) pecan nuts
100 g (3½ oz) plain flour
60 g (2 oz) low fat spread

1 Spray a medium non stick pan with the cooking spray and cook the onion and garlic for 2–3 minutes.

2 Add the celery, carrots, tomatoes and baby corn. Stir well. Cook for 3–4 minutes.

3 Stir in the lentils and chick peas then pour over the stock. Season and bring to a simmer. Continue to simmer for 15 minutes.

4 Preheat the oven to Gas Mark 6/200°C/fan oven 180°C.

5 Meanwhile, place the nuts and flour in a food processor and whizz for a few seconds to chop up the nuts. Add the low fat spread and whizz until the mixture resembles chunky breadcrumbs.

6 Pour the chick pea and vegetable mixture into a baking dish and spoon over the crumble. Bake in the oven for 15–20 minutes until golden.

8 **ProPoints** values per serving
49 **ProPoints** values per recipe

C 325 **calories** per serving

Takes **20 minutes** to prepare, **15–20 minutes** to cook

V

✳ recommended for up to **1 month**

Variation Crumble 50 g (1¾ oz) of Stilton and stir it into the topping before spooning it over the vegetables. The **ProPoints** values per serving will be 10.

Spicy Tofu Courgettes

A quick and tasty dish for two.

Serves 2

calorie controlled cooking spray
2 garlic cloves, crushed
2 cm (¾ inch) fresh root ginger,
   finely chopped
1 star anise
2 courgettes, sliced thickly

2 spring onions, sliced
1 teaspoon cornflour
125 ml (4 fl oz) vegetable stock
125 g (4½ oz) tofu, cut into cubes
salt and freshly ground black
   pepper

1　Heat a non stick frying pan or wok, spray with the cooking spray
and stir fry the garlic and ginger for 1–2 minutes. Add the star anise,
courgettes and spring onions and fry for 1 minute.

2　Place the cornflour in a small bowl or cup and stir in 1 tablespoon of
the stock to make a smooth paste – leave to one side.

3　Pour the remaining stock into the wok or frying pan, season and
bring to a simmer. Cook for 4–5 minutes.

4　Remove the courgettes with a slotted spoon, then add the tofu to the
pan. Cook for 2–3 minutes before pouring in the cornflour mixture.
Stir well until the mixture thickens then return the courgettes to the
pan. Check the seasoning and serve.

2 ProPoints values per serving
5 ProPoints values per recipe

95 calories per serving

Takes **5 minutes** to prepare,
12 minutes to cook

V

＊　not recommended

Tip Tofu is the Japanese name for bean curd – a pale soft cheese-like
substance that is made from soya bean milk.

Variation Other zero **ProPoints** value vegetables can be used – try
broccoli or carrots.

Sweet Potato Stew

Based on an African recipe, this mildly curried hearty vegetable stew is thickened and flavoured with reduced fat peanut butter, which gives the sauce a rich, velvety texture.

Serves 4

calorie controlled cooking spray

1 large onion, chopped roughly

3 mixed peppers, de-seeded and chopped roughly

2 tablespoons medium curry powder

500 g (1 lb 2 oz) sweet potatoes, peeled and diced

400 ml (14 fl oz) boiling water

60 g (2 oz) reduced fat peanut butter

2 tablespoons fresh coriander, chopped

salt and freshly ground black pepper

---

6 ProPoints values per serving
24 ProPoints values per recipe

C **245 calories** per serving

Takes **25 minutes**

V

✳ not recommended

1 Lightly spray a lidded, flameproof casserole dish with the cooking spray, add the onion and peppers and stir fry for 5 minutes until browned.

2 Stir in the curry powder and sweet potatoes and toss to coat everything in the spices.

3 Add the boiling water then stir in the peanut butter. Bring to a simmer, season, cover and cook for 12 minutes until tender. Stir in the coriander just before serving and ladle the stew into warm bowls.

Gnocchi with a Quick Tomato Sauce

Gnocchi are Italian potato dumplings and they're ideal for a quick and filling supper.

Serves 4

400 g (14 oz) fresh gnocchi
40 g (1½ oz) Parmesan cheese, grated
a handful of fresh basil leaves, torn, to garnish

For the tomato sauce

1 large onion, chopped finely
1 tablespoon tomato purée
2 x 400 g cans chopped tomatoes with chilli
300 ml (10 fl oz) vegetable stock
1 teaspoon sugar
salt and freshly ground black pepper

6 ProPoints values per serving
22 ProPoints values per recipe

230 calories per serving

Takes **30 minutes**

V

✷ recommended (sauce only)

1 To make the sauce, place all the ingredients in a saucepan. Bring to the boil and simmer uncovered for 20 minutes, until the liquid has been reduced to a thick pulpy sauce. Season to taste.

2 Meanwhile, bring a pan of water to the boil, add the gnocchi and cook according to the packet instructions. Drain thoroughly. Preheat the grill to high.

3 Spoon a little sauce in the base of four shallow, flameproof bowls. Add the gnocchi and pour over the remaining sauce. Sprinkle on the Parmesan cheese. Grill for 2 minutes, until the cheese turns golden brown.

4 Scatter the basil leaves over and serve immediately.

Tip This sauce is such a good base for so many dishes; it's excellent with grilled vegetables or pasta. Make up a batch and freeze handy portion sizes to use later.

Variations For special occasions, replace 150 ml (5 fl oz) of the stock with red wine. Remember to add 1 **ProPoints** value per serving.

Add 225 g (8 oz) of chopped mushrooms, or 1 fiery hot chopped chilli and some chopped fresh coriander. The **ProPoints** values will remain the same.

Spring Vegetable Cobbler

Serves 6

calorie controlled cooking spray

a bunch of spring onions, chopped

150 g (5½ oz) low fat soft cheese with garlic and herbs

300 ml (10 fl oz) vegetable stock

200 g (7 oz) baby carrots, scrubbed, tops trimmed and chopped finely

200 g (7 oz) baby turnips, scrubbed, tops trimmed and chopped finely

200 g (7 oz) frozen petit pois

200 g (7 oz) frozen sweetcorn

200 g (7 oz) sugar snap peas

1 head of broccoli, cut into small florets

For the topping

150 g (5½ oz) self raising flour

1 teaspoon baking powder

a small bunch of fresh parsley or coriander, chopped finely

1 teaspoon dried oregano or herbes de Provence

½ teaspoon English mustard powder

40 g (1½ oz) low fat spread, melted

100 ml (3½ fl oz) skimmed milk

salt and freshly ground black pepper

6 ProPoints values per serving
33 ProPoints values per recipe

249 calories per serving

Takes **35 minutes** to prepare,
25 minutes to cook

V

✳ not recommended

1 Preheat the oven to Gas Mark 6/200°C/fan oven 180°C. Spray a large, flameproof casserole dish with the cooking spray and then fry the spring onions, until golden.

2 Add the soft cheese and stock and stir until smooth. Add all the vegetables and mix, so that they are covered in the sauce.

3 To make the topping, mix the flour, baking powder, fresh and dried herbs, mustard and seasoning together in a bowl. Pour the low fat spread into the centre. Add the milk and quickly mix together with a wooden spoon – don't overmix it.

4 Using two dessertspoons, spoon the scone mixture into six mounds or cobbles around the edge of the casserole dish, leaving gaps in the middle for the vegetables to show through.

5 Bake for 25 minutes, until the top is risen and golden and the sauce is bubbling hot underneath.

Quorn au Vin

Serve this tasty vegetarian version of Coq au Vin with lightly cooked vegetables, such as broccoli, carrots and green beans, and 200 g (7 oz) boiled new potatoes per person, for an extra 4 *ProPoints* values per serving.

Serves 4

calorie controlled cooking spray
2 onions, chopped
1 garlic clove, crushed
200 g (7 oz) diced Quorn
200 g (7 oz) mushrooms, sliced
350 ml (12 fl oz) hot vegetable stock
200 ml (7 fl oz) red wine
1 tablespoon tomato purée
1 teaspoon dried mixed herbs
1 tablespoon cornflour
2 tablespoons chopped fresh parsley
salt and freshly ground black pepper

3 *ProPoints* values per serving
13 *ProPoints* values per recipe

120 calories per serving

Takes 45 minutes

V

✳ recommended

1 Spray the base of a large non stick saucepan with the cooking spray. Heat for a few moments, then sauté the onions and garlic until golden, about 5–6 minutes.

2 Add the Quorn and mushrooms and cook, stirring, for 2–3 more minutes. Add the stock and wine, then bring to the boil. Reduce the heat and simmer until the liquid has reduced by approximately one third.

3 Stir in the tomato purée and herbs. Season to taste, then simmer for 10–15 minutes more.

4 Blend the cornflour with a little cold water and add to the saucepan, stirring until thickened. Add the chopped parsley, then serve.

Tip Prepare this dish the day before to allow the flavours to mellow and intensify. Re-heat thoroughly in the oven or microwave.

Stuffed Field Mushrooms

Serve these tasty mushrooms with a zero *ProPoints* value crunchy salad of shredded cos or Little Gem lettuce, cucumber and grated raw carrot.

Serves 2

100 g (3½ oz) dried couscous
400 ml (14 fl oz) vegetable stock
4 large (or 6–8 medium) field mushrooms, cleaned
100 g (3½ oz) light Feta cheese, diced
a small bunch of fresh thyme, woody stems removed, chopped
100 ml (3½ fl oz) passata
freshly ground black pepper

---

7 *ProPoints* values per serving
15 *ProPoints* values per recipe

286 calories per serving

Takes **15 minutes** to prepare,
20 minutes to cook

V

✳ not recommended

1 Place the couscous in a bowl and pour over 200 ml (7 fl oz) of the stock. Cover and leave to soak for 5 minutes.

2 Preheat the oven to Gas Mark 4/180°C/fan oven 160°C. Remove the stalks from the mushrooms and chop finely. Set aside. Place the whole mushrooms, tops down, in an ovenproof dish or baking tray.

3 Remove the cover from the couscous and add the chopped mushroom stalks, Feta cheese, thyme, passata and plenty of black pepper. Stir with a fork.

4 Pile the couscous mixture into the mushrooms and pour the remaining 200 ml (7 fl oz) of stock around them.

5 Bake for 20 minutes or until golden brown.

Tip Prepare the mushrooms and couscous mixture the night before and keep them in the fridge. All you have to do is add the last 200 ml (7 fl oz) of stock and pop it in the oven when you get home.

Variations Use your favourite herbs in this recipe, such as basil, parsley, dried Mediterranean herbs or mint, instead of thyme.

Mince Parcels

Choose large Iceberg lettuce leaves to wrap up this spicy filling.

Serves 4

1 tablespoon chilli oil
1 garlic clove, crushed
350 g (12 oz) frozen soy mince, thawed
225 g (8 oz) courgettes, grated
1 teaspoon ground coriander
1 teaspoon cumin seeds
1 tablespoon tomato purée
¼ kettleful of boiling water

To serve

4 tablespoons sweet chilli sauce
a bowl of fresh lettuce leaves

---

4 ProPoints values per serving
15 ProPoints values per recipe

C **175 calories** per serving

Takes **20 minutes**

V

✳ recommended (filling only)

1 Heat the chilli oil in a non stick frying pan, add the garlic and soy mince and cook for 5 minutes.

2 Stir in the courgettes, coriander, cumin, tomato purée and 4 tablespoons of boiling water. Cook for a further 5 minutes.

3 To serve, pile into a warmed serving dish, and let everyone 'build' their own parcels at the table by drizzling a little chilli sauce on to a lettuce leaf and then spooning some mince mixture into the centre. Wrap up, enclosing the filling.

Tip You can flavour your own oils at home. Just place a few chillies in a screw top jar, add enough olive oil to cover and leave to soak for at least 1 month to take up the flavour of the chillies.

Tasty Noodles and Vegetables

A light, fragrant meal that can be on the table in minutes.

Serves 4

250 g (9 oz) dried noodles
calorie controlled cooking spray
2 garlic cloves, sliced finely
2.5 cm (1 inch) fresh root ginger, diced finely
1 head of broccoli, cut into florets
2 red peppers, de-seeded and cut into bite size pieces
100 g (3½ oz) baby corn, cut into bite size pieces
2 tablespoons plum sauce
150 ml (5 fl oz) vegetable stock
1 packet fresh coriander or parsley, chopped

8 ProPoints values per serving
30 ProPoints values per recipe

C **300 calories** per serving

Takes **10 minutes** to prepare,
10 minutes to cook

V

* not recommended

1 Bring a pan of water to the boil, add the noodles and cook according to the packet instructions. Drain.

2 Spray a large non stick frying pan or wok with the cooking spray and put it on a high heat. Stir fry the garlic and ginger for 2 minutes, then add the vegetables and stir fry for another 4 minutes or until they have started to brown at the edges.

3 Add the plum sauce and stock and bring to the boil.

4 Stir in the noodles and fresh coriander or parsley and serve.

Vegetable Pilaff

A delicious and filling meal, full of fabulous flavours and vegetables.

Serves 4

calorie controlled cooking spray
1 large onion, chopped
1 garlic clove, crushed
1 leek, sliced
1 red pepper, de-seeded and sliced
1 courgette, sliced
75 g (2¾ oz) baby corn, halved
110 g (4 oz) asparagus tips
1 teaspoon ground cumin
1 teaspoon turmeric
a large pinch of saffron threads
180 g (6½ oz) dried long grain or basmati rice
500 ml (18 fl oz) vegetable stock

To garnish
30 g (1¼ oz) flaked almonds
½ teaspoon chilli powder

6 ProPoints values per serving
23 ProPoints values per recipe

265 calories per serving

Takes **30 minutes** to prepare,
20 minutes to cook

V

✳ recommended for up to **1 month**

1 Spray a very large, lidded, non stick frying pan with the cooking spray. Add the onion, garlic and leek and cook for 3–4 minutes until they start to soften. Add the pepper, courgette, baby corn and asparagus and cook for another 3–4 minutes before adding the spices and saffron.

2 Add the rice and stir well to coat everything in the spices.

3 Pour in the stock, bring to a simmer and cover. Simmer for 20 minutes until all the liquid has been absorbed and the rice is cooked.

4 Meanwhile, spray a small non stick frying pan with the cooking spray and stir fry the flaked almonds and chilli powder for 5–6 minutes until they are golden. Set aside on kitchen towel.

5 When the pilaff is cooked, transfer it to a large serving plate or dish and sprinkle with the spicy almond flakes.

Tip Make sure the frying pan is covered completely to help the rice to steam – try not to remove the cover for a look too often.

Variations Most zero **ProPoints** value vegetables can be used for this dish; try broccoli, cauliflower and celery, or even root vegetables like swede and turnip.

Family Favourites

Replace your family favourites with these equally delicious vegetarian versions. Try Spicy Bean Burgers, Vegetable Lasagne, Leek and Mushroom Pie or Garlic Mushroom and Goat's Cheese Pizza.

All the family will love these great supper dishes

Zesty Grilled Peppers and Courgette Mini Pizzas

The whole family will love this colourful tasty pizza – perfect at the end of the week.

Makes 4 mini pizzas

calorie controlled cooking spray
2 red peppers, de-seeded and cut into thin wedges
2 courgettes, sliced
4 x 10 cm (4 inch) ready made pizza bases
225 g (8 oz) low fat soft cheese
1 garlic clove, crushed
grated zest and juice of a lemon
salt and freshly ground black pepper

---

8 ProPoints values per serving
30 ProPoints values per recipe

340 calories per serving

Takes **10 minutes** to prepare,
10–15 minutes to cook

V

✳ not recommended

1 Preheat the oven to Gas Mark 9/240°C/fan oven 220°C and preheat the grill to high.

2 Spray a baking sheet with the cooking spray and put the vegetables on it. Place the vegetables under the grill for 5 minutes or until they have started to blacken.

3 Meanwhile, spread the pizza bases with the soft cheese.

4 Put the hot grilled vegetables in a bowl and toss with the garlic, lemon zest and juice. Season. Pile on to the pizza bases and bake in the oven for 10–15 minutes or until the bases are crisp and golden.

Garden Paella

This is a vibrant variation on the Spanish favourite.

6 ProPoints value

Serves 8

calorie controlled cooking spray

3 garlic cloves, crushed

2 red peppers, de-seeded and diced finely

450 g (1 lb) tomatoes, chopped

a generous pinch of saffron strands, soaked in 2 tablespoons of boiling water for 5 minutes

½ teaspoon paprika or cayenne pepper

a small bunch of fresh thyme, woody stems removed, leaves chopped

400 g (14 oz) dried long grain or basmati rice

1.2 litres (2 pints) vegetable stock

2 bay leaves

450 g (1 lb) small courgettes, sliced thinly and diagonally

225 g (8 oz) frozen or fresh peas

225 g (8 oz) green beans

a bunch of spring onions, chopped

grated zest and juice of a lemon

salt and freshly ground black pepper

1 lemon, cut into 8 wedges, to serve

---

6 ProPoints values per serving
44 ProPoints values per recipe

257 calories per serving

Takes **20 minutes** to prepare, **25 minutes** to cook

V

✳ not recommended

1 Heat a large, lidded, non stick frying pan or wok and spray with the cooking spray. Stir fry the garlic and peppers for 5 minutes or until golden and softened.

2 Add the tomatoes, saffron strands and soaking water, spices, thyme, rice, stock, bay leaves and 100 ml (3½ fl oz) of water. Stir together. Cover and cook for 10 minutes.

3 Stir the rice and then pile all the remaining vegetables with the lemon zest and juice and seasoning on top. Replace the lid and cook for a further 10 minutes. Uncover and stir.

4 Remove the bay leaves and serve with lemon wedges.

Macaroni Cheese

This inexpensive and nutritious dish is a family favourite.

Serves 4

175 g (6 oz) dried macaroni
2 tablespoons low fat spread
40 g (1½ oz) plain flour
450 ml (15 fl oz) skimmed milk
175 g (6 oz) half fat Cheddar cheese
a good pinch of mustard powder
3 tomatoes, sliced
15 g (½ oz) fresh breadcrumbs
salt and freshly ground black pepper

10 *ProPoints* values per serving
41 *ProPoints* values per recipe

389 calories per serving

Takes **10 minutes** to prepare,
20 minutes to cook

V

✱ recommended

1 Bring a pan of water to the boil, add the pasta and cook for about 10 minutes, or according to the packet instructions, until just tender.

2 Meanwhile, put the low fat spread, flour and milk into a saucepan. Heat, stirring constantly with a small whisk, until the sauce boils and thickens. Reduce the heat and cook gently for a couple of minutes. Remove from the heat.

3 Preheat the grill. Stir about two thirds of the cheese into the sauce and allow it to melt. Season with the mustard powder and seasoning. Drain the pasta thoroughly and add it to the sauce, stirring to coat. Transfer the mixture to a 1.5 litre (2¾ pints) flameproof dish.

4 Arrange the sliced tomatoes over the surface, then sprinkle with the breadcrumbs and remaining cheese. Grill until browned and bubbling.

Variation Use penne (pasta tubes) instead of macaroni if you prefer, or any type of pasta shape that will hold the cheese sauce. The *ProPoints* values will remain the same.

Shepherdess Pie

This is an ideal dish to freeze in individual portions and defrost as necessary.

Serves 4

calorie controlled cooking spray
1 leek, washed and chopped finely
1 small courgette, diced
1 carrot, peeled and diced
1 garlic clove, crushed
110 g (4 oz) mushrooms, sliced
60 g (2 oz) dried red lentils
60 g (2 oz) dried green lentils
225 g can chopped tomatoes
1 bay leaf
½ teaspoon dried marjoram
½ teaspoon dried thyme
1½ tablespoons brown sauce
220 g can baked beans
salt and freshly ground black pepper

For the topping

900 g (2 lb) potatoes, peeled and halved if large
5–6 tablespoons skimmed milk
25 g (1 oz) half fat Cheddar cheese, grated

10 ProPoints values per serving
38 ProPoints values per recipe

258 calories per serving

Takes **15–20 minutes** to prepare,
1 hour 10 minutes to cook

V

✱ recommended

1 Preheat the oven to Gas Mark 6/200°C/fan oven 180°C.

2 Spray a large, lidded, non stick pan with the cooking spray then gently fry the leek, courgette, carrot, garlic and mushrooms for 10 minutes, adding a splash of water if the vegetables start to stick.

3 Add the lentils, tomatoes, bay leaf, herbs and 450 ml (16 fl oz) of water. Bring the mixture to the boil then reduce the heat. Partially cover the pan and simmer for 30 minutes or until the lentils are soft and the mixture is thick. Stir in the brown sauce and baked beans then cook for a further 5 minutes.

4 Meanwhile, make the topping. Place the potatoes in a pan of water, bring to the boil then simmer for about 20 minutes until tender. Drain the potatoes, return to the pan then heat gently to dry out. Mash the potatoes with the milk and seasoning.

5 Remove the bay leaf from the lentil mixture and check the seasoning. Spoon the mixture into a large, ovenproof dish. Pile the mash on top and fork it over. Sprinkle with the grated cheese.

6 Bake in the oven for 15–20 minutes or until the potato is crispy. Serve immediately.

Sausage Casserole with Leek and Onion Mash

This recipe can be prepared quickly in the morning and then left in the slow cooker.

Serves 4

250 g packet Quorn sausages
2–3 carrots, peeled and chopped
1 large onion, chopped
1 garlic clove, crushed
415 g can baked beans
400 g can chopped tomatoes
1 teaspoon dried mixed herbs
salt and freshly ground black pepper

For the mash

1 large leek, washed and chopped
a bunch of spring onions, chopped
4 x 200 g (7 oz) potatoes, cut into chunks

9 *ProPoints* values per serving
35 *ProPoints* values per recipe

365 calories per serving

Takes **20 minutes** to prepare,
1¼ hours to cook

V

✳ recommended (casserole only)

1 Preheat the oven (if using) to Gas Mark 2/150°C/fan oven 130°C.

2 Slice each sausage in half, then place all the casserole ingredients in a flameproof casserole dish with 200 ml (7 fl oz) of water. Place the dish on the hob and bring the mixture to the boil. Then either transfer to the oven for an hour or turn the heat down low and leave it on the hob for an hour.

3 Half an hour before you are ready to eat, place the leek, spring onions and potatoes in a large pan with enough water just to cover them. Bring to the boil and cook for 20 minutes or until tender. Drain and mash together with some seasoning. Serve the casserole with the leek and onion mash.

Tip To reduce the *ProPoints* values, replace the baked beans with zero *ProPoints* value vegetables such as celery, celeriac, cabbage, brussels sprouts, swede or turnips. This will reduce the *ProPoints* values to 6 per serving.

Creamy Vegetable and Chick Pea Korma

This mild korma is perfumed with aromatic spices rather than being heavy on chilli. The combination of sweet butternut squash and succulent peppers with the nuttiness of the chick peas is simply divine.

Serves 4

2 teaspoons sunflower oil
1 onion, sliced
2 red peppers, de-seeded and chopped
1 butternut squash, peeled, de-seeded and diced
2 garlic cloves, crushed
1 tablespoon grated fresh root ginger
1 tablespoon ground coriander
1 teaspoon cumin seeds
a pinch of hot chilli powder
25 g (1 oz) ground almonds
250 ml (9 fl oz) vegetable stock
200 ml (7 fl oz) reduced fat coconut milk
110 g (4 oz) green beans, trimmed and cut
   into thirds
410 g can chick peas, drained and rinsed
salt and freshly ground black pepper

5 ProPoints values per serving
21 ProPoints values per recipe

317 calories per serving

Takes **20 minutes** to prepare,
25 minutes to cook

V

✳ not recommended

1 Heat the oil in a large, lidded, non stick pan. Fry the onion and peppers over a medium heat for 5 minutes.

2 Add the butternut squash, garlic, ginger and spices and stir until evenly coated. Add the ground almonds, then blend in the vegetable stock and coconut milk. Season to taste then bring to the boil, cover and simmer for 15 minutes.

3 Add the green beans and chick peas and cook for a further 10 minutes. Serve immediately.

Mexican Tacos

A simple dressing of chilli oil, lime juice and vinegar spices up this Mexican inspired salad. Serve it packed into crispy taco shells.

Serves 4

40 g (1½ oz) dried long grain rice
2 tablespoons lime or lemon juice
1 tablespoon chilli oil
1 tablespoon white wine or cider vinegar
1 small avocado, peeled, stoned and chopped
1 small red onion, finely chopped
½ green pepper, de-seeded and chopped
2 tomatoes, chopped
2 tablespoons chopped fresh coriander or
  parsley, plus extra to garnish
215 g can red kidney beans, drained and rinsed
8 taco shells
salt and freshly ground black pepper

1 Bring a pan of water to the boil, add the rice and cook according to the packet instructions. Drain and allow to cool.

2 Preheat the oven to Gas Mark 1/140°C/ fan oven 120°C. In a large bowl, whisk together the lime or lemon juice, chilli oil and vinegar.

3 Add the avocado, onion, pepper, tomatoes, chopped coriander or parsley, rice and kidney beans. Stir well and season to taste.

4 Warm the taco shells in the oven for a few minutes, then pack with the rice mixture and serve at once, garnished with coriander or parsley.

9 *ProPoints* values per serving
35 *ProPoints* values per recipe

265 calories per serving

Takes **40 minutes**

V

✳ not recommend

Tip Use olive oil if you don't have any chilli oil, then season the rice mixture with a dash of chilli sauce. The *ProPoints* values will remain the same.

Sweet and Sour Quorn

A quick and easy sweet and sour stir fry, using just a handful of ingredients. Serve with 40 g (1½ oz) of dried rice per person, cooked according to packet instructions, adding an extra 6 **ProPoints** values per serving.

Serves 4

2 tablespoons cornflour
4 tablespoons tomato ketchup
432 g can pineapple cubes
   in natural juice
calorie controlled cooking spray
300 g packet Quorn Chicken
   Style Pieces

a bunch of spring onions, cut
   into chunks
3 mixed peppers, de-seeded
   and chopped roughly

1 Blend the cornflour with 150 ml (5 fl oz) of cold water in a jug, then whisk in the tomato ketchup and the juice from the canned pineapple.

2 Heat a large non stick frying pan or wok on the hob, spray with the cooking spray and stir fry the Quorn pieces for 2 minutes. Add the spring onions and peppers and continue to cook, stirring, for 3–4 minutes. Pour in the sauce and simmer the mixture for 5 minutes, then stir in the cubes of pineapple and heat through for 2 minutes before serving.

5 ProPoints values per serving
20 ProPoints values per recipe

C **198 calories** per serving

Takes **20 minutes**

V

✱ not recommended

Leek and Mushroom Pie

Crisp cheese and herb pastry acts as a delicious contrast to the flavoursome filling in this satisfying dish. The pie is great served with zero *ProPoints* value vegetables.

Serves 4

For the pastry

150 g (5½ oz) plain flour, sifted, plus 1 teaspoon for rolling
a pinch of salt
80 g (3 oz) low fat spread
15 g (½ oz) fresh Parmesan cheese, grated
1 tablespoon chopped fresh thyme
freshly ground black pepper

For the filling

50 g (1¾ oz) low fat spread
4 large leeks, washed, trimmed and sliced
300 ml (10 fl oz) vegetable stock
450 g (1 lb) mushrooms, quartered or halved
40 g (1½ oz) plain flour
300 ml (10 fl oz) skimmed milk
1 tablespoon wholegrain mustard

9 *ProPoints* values per serving
38 *ProPoints* values per recipe

392 calories per serving

Takes **35 minutes** to prepare,
30 minutes to cook

V

✳ not recommended

1 Preheat the oven to Gas Mark 5/190°C/fan oven 170°C.

2 To make the pastry, sift the flour into a bowl with a pinch of salt and freshly ground black pepper. Rub in the low fat spread until the mixture is crumbly, then stir in the Parmesan cheese and thyme. Add enough cold water to bring the pastry together into a smooth ball. Shape into a disc, wrap in cling film and chill for 30 minutes.

3 To start making the filling, melt 2 teaspoons of low fat spread in a lidded non stick saucepan. Stir in the leeks and 2 tablespoons of stock, cover and cook for 5 minutes until tender, then transfer to a lipped ceramic pie dish.

4 Put the mushrooms and 2 tablespoons of stock into the same saucepan and cook, covered, for 5 minutes. Lift the mushrooms into the pie dish using a slotted spoon, increase the heat under the saucepan and cook the remaining liquid for about 3 minutes until reduced by half, then pour into the pie dish.

5 Now add the remaining low fat spread, stock, plain flour and milk to the saucepan. Bring to the boil, whisking until smooth. Simmer for 3 minutes then stir in the mustard and seasoning to taste. Pour over the leeks and mushrooms in the pie dish.

6 Dust the work surface with 1 teaspoon of flour and roll out the pastry thinly. Cut a narrow strip of pastry and press on to the rim of the pie dish. Brush with water, lift the pastry lid on top and press around the edge with a fork to seal the edges. Trim away any excess pastry.

7 Bake the pie for 30 minutes until crisp and golden.

Tofu and Vegetable Kebabs

Use your favourite vegetables to make colourful kebabs for a summer barbecue.

Serves 4

50 ml (2 fl oz) soy sauce
1 garlic clove, crushed
2.5 cm (1 inch) fresh root ginger, chopped
1 teaspoon Tabasco sauce
250 g (9 oz) firm tofu, cut into large cubes
16 cherry tomatoes
1 red pepper, de-seeded and chopped
1 yellow pepper, de-seeded and chopped
1 red onion, cut into 8 chunks
8 large mushrooms, halved

2 **ProPoints** values per serving
7 **ProPoints** values per recipe

98 **calories** per serving

Takes **30 minutes** + **2 hours** marinating

V

✳ not recommended

1 Mix together the soy sauce, garlic, ginger, Tabasco sauce and 4½ tablespoons of water. Place the tofu in the marinade and leave for at least 2 hours or preferably overnight in the fridge.

2 Preheat the grill to high. Soak eight wooden kebab skewers in water for 10 minutes to prevent them from burning. Thread the vegetables and tofu on to the kebab skewers and cook under the hot grill or over a barbecue for 10–15 minutes, turning regularly, until the vegetables are starting to char at the edges.

Pasta Ratatouille

This classic sauce from France is perfect with pasta.

Serves 4

350 g (12 oz) dried pasta
1 packet fresh basil, chopped (optional)

For the ratatouille
calorie controlled cooking spray
2 onions, chopped roughly
2 garlic cloves, chopped roughly
1 large aubergine, cubed
4 courgettes, sliced
2 green peppers, de-seeded and sliced
400 g can chopped tomatoes with herbs
leaves from 3 sprigs of fresh thyme or rosemary
 or 1 teaspoon dried thyme or rosemary
1 teaspoon sugar
salt and freshly ground black pepper

9 *ProPoints* values per serving
35 *ProPoints* values per recipe

400 calories per serving

Takes **30 minutes** to prepare,
45 minutes to cook

V

✳ not recommended

1 Spray a large non stick pan with the cooking spray and put on a medium heat. Add the onions and garlic and cook for 4 minutes, until softened.

2 Add the other ratatouille ingredients, season and simmer for 45 minutes or until reduced and thickened.

3 Meanwhile, bring a pan of water to the boil, add the pasta and cook according to the packet instructions or until tender. Drain.

4 Check the sauce for seasoning, toss with the pasta and serve sprinkled with fresh basil, if using.

Spinach Cannelloni

This delicious recipe has been adapted from the classic Italian dish.

Serves 4

400 g (14 oz) spinach, washed
calorie controlled cooking spray
1 onion, chopped finely
2 garlic cloves, chopped finely
¼ teaspoon grated nutmeg
a bunch of fresh basil leaves, chopped roughly,
   reserving a few leaves to garnish
16 quick cook cannelloni tubes
1 tablespoon grated Parmesan cheese

For the topping

2 teaspoons cornflour
450 ml (16 fl oz) low fat natural yogurt
100 g (3½ oz) low fat soft cheese
salt and freshly ground black pepper

7 *ProPoints* values per serving
28 *ProPoints* values per recipe

445 calories per serving

Takes **25 minutes** to prepare,
45 minutes to cook

V

✳ not recommended

1 Put the spinach in a large lidded pan and cover. Cook gently for 10 minutes, stirring occasionally, until wilted but not dry.

2 Preheat the oven to Gas Mark 4/180°C/fan oven 160°C. Spray a pan with the cooking spray and sauté the onion and garlic gently for 4 minutes or until softened, adding a tablespoon of water if they stick.

3 Add the spinach, nutmeg and most of the basil. Mix together. Put this mixture to one side to cool a little.

4 For the topping, mix the cornflour with 1 tablespoon of water to make a paste, then beat together with the yogurt and soft cheese to obtain a thick and creamy consistency. Season to taste.

5 Stuff the cannelloni with the spinach mixture using a teaspoon. Put in an ovenproof dish tightly packed together. Spoon over the topping and sprinkle with the Parmesan cheese.

6 Bake for 45 minutes until the top is golden and the cannelloni cooked. Sprinkle with fresh basil leaves to serve.

Tip Instead of fresh spinach, you could use frozen, defrosted spinach. There is no need to blanch it, just squeeze out any excess water and chop it.

Garlic Mushroom and Goat's Cheese Pizza

Serve with a mixed zero *ProPoints* value salad, dressed with a little balsamic vinegar.

Serves 4

300 g (10½ oz) plain flour
2 teaspoons fast action yeast
1 teaspoon salt
2 teaspoons olive oil
calorie controlled cooking spray
300 g (10½ oz) small dark gilled mushrooms, halved
2 garlic cloves, crushed
100 g (3½ oz) passata
1 tablespoon fresh thyme leaves
75 g (2¾ oz) mild soft goat's cheese
freshly ground black pepper

10 *ProPoints* values per serving
38 *ProPoints* values per recipe

341 calories per serving

Takes **15 minutes** to prepare
+ **1 hour 10 minutes** rising,
15 minutes to cook

V

✻ not recommended

1 Sift all but 3 teaspoons of the flour into a mixing bowl. Stir in the yeast and salt. Make a well in the centre and add the olive oil. Mix in about 200 ml (7 fl oz) of warm water, or just enough to bring the mixture together to form a soft, but not sticky, dough.

2 Dust the work surface with 2 teaspoons of the reserved flour and turn out the dough on to the floured surface. Knead for 3 minutes until smooth. Return to the bowl, cover with cling film and leave to rise in a warm place for 1 hour, or until doubled in size.

3 Preheat the oven to Gas Mark 7/220°C/fan oven 200°C. Spray a lidded non stick pan with the cooking spray. Add the mushrooms, garlic and 1 tablespoon of water. Season with black pepper. Cover and cook for 3–4 minutes until juicy. Cook for a further 1–2 minutes with the lid off to evaporate the juices, then leave to cool.

4 Dust the work surface with the remaining 1 teaspoon of flour and roll out the pizza base to fit a 20 x 30 cm (8 x 12 inch) baking sheet. Transfer the rolled base to the baking sheet.

5 Spread the base with the passata and scatter on half the thyme. Top with the mushrooms and dot with small clumps of the goat's cheese.

6 Leave to rise for 10 minutes, then bake for 15 minutes until well risen and crisp. Scatter with the remaining thyme just before serving and cut into quarters.

Moroccan Stew

The aubergines soak up the flavours beautifully in this Moroccan spiced stew. The squash adds a little sweetness, which is so well enhanced by the cinnamon.

Serves 4

1 tablespoon olive oil
1 onion, sliced
1 garlic clove, crushed
1 large aubergine, diced
225 g (8 oz) carrots, peeled and sliced
350 g (12 oz) butternut squash, peeled, de-seeded and diced
1 teaspoon ground cinnamon
1 teaspoon ground cumin
1 teaspoon ground coriander
2 tablespoons tomato purée
300 ml (10 fl oz) vegetable stock
200 g (7 oz) silken tofu, cubed
50 g (1¾ oz) no-soak dried apricots, chopped
2 tablespoons chopped fresh coriander
1 teaspoon chopped fresh mint
salt and freshly ground black pepper
25 g (1 oz) toasted pine nut kernels (see Tip), to garnish

5 ProPoints values per serving
18 ProPoints values per recipe

C **225 calories** per serving

Takes **25 minutes** to prepare, **50 minutes** to cook

V

✳ recommended

1 Heat the olive oil in a large, lidded, heatproof casserole dish and add the onion, garlic, aubergine, carrots and squash. Cook, stirring, for 5 minutes. Add the cinnamon, cumin, coriander and seasoning and cook for a further minute.

2 Add the tomato purée and stock. Bring to the boil, cover and simmer for 40 minutes, stirring from time to time.

3 Add the tofu, apricots, fresh coriander and mint and cook for a further 5 minutes.

4 Just before serving, scatter the toasted pine nut kernels over the top.

Tip Toasting pine kernels before adding them to dishes gives them a richer flavour so you can get away with using less. Heat a small heavy based or non stick pan and add the pine nut kernels. Cook over a gentle heat for about 2 minutes, tossing constantly until they brown a little. Take care because once they begin to brown, they will do so very quickly.

Spaghetti Bolognese

A favourite Italian recipe.

Serves 4

calorie controlled cooking spray
1 onion, finely chopped
150 g (5½ oz) mushrooms, sliced
2 garlic cloves, crushed
350 g packet Quorn mince
½ teaspoon dried mixed herbs
1 tablespoon tomato purée
400 g can chopped tomatoes
250 g (9 oz) dried spaghetti
salt and freshly ground black pepper

8 ProPoints values per serving
33 ProPoints values per recipe

332 calories per serving

Takes **15 minutes** to prepare,
15 minutes to cook

V

✳ recommended (sauce only)

1 Spray a non stick frying pan with the cooking spray. Add the onion and cook for 5 minutes until softened and lightly browned, adding a splash of water, if needed, to prevent it from sticking.

2 Stir in the mushrooms, garlic and seasoning and cook for a further 2 minutes. Add the Quorn mince, herbs, tomato purée and tomatoes, bring to a simmer and cook for 12–15 minutes.

3 Meanwhile, bring a large pan of water to the boil, add the pasta and cook for 10–12 minutes until al dente.

4 Drain the pasta and serve in warmed bowls, with the sauce ladled over the top.

Vegetable Chow Mein

Egg noodles only take a few minutes to prepare, so combine them with stir fried vegetables to make a quick and tasty Chinese style supper.

Serves 4

3 tablespoons light soy sauce
1 tablespoon rice vinegar or white wine vinegar
1 large green chilli, de-seeded and sliced finely
1 teaspoon finely grated fresh root ginger
2 tablespoons chopped fresh coriander or parsley
1 teaspoon Chinese five spice
250 g (9 oz) firm tofu, cubed
175 g (6 oz) dried medium egg noodles
a kettleful of boiling water
2 teaspoons vegetable oil
a bunch of spring onions, chopped
1 carrot, peeled and cut into fine strips
3 celery sticks, chopped
¼ cucumber, de-seeded and sliced
75 g (2¾ oz) fresh beansprouts
salt and freshly ground black pepper
fresh coriander or parsley sprigs, to garnish

7 ProPoints values per serving
30 ProPoints values per recipe

285 calories per serving

Takes **25 minutes** to prepare,
+ **1–2 hours** marinating

V

✳ not recommended

1 Put the soy sauce, vinegar, chilli, ginger, coriander or parsley and Chinese five spice into a non metallic bowl. Stir well and then add the tofu cubes. Cover and leave to marinate for 1–2 hours, or overnight if preferred.

2 Soak the egg noodles in the boiling water for about 6 minutes, or according to the packet instructions.

3 Heat the oil in a wok or large frying pan and add the spring onions, carrot, celery and cucumber. Stir fry for 2–3 minutes. Add the tofu with its marinade and then the beansprouts. Stir fry for another 2 minutes.

4 Drain the noodles thoroughly and add them to the wok or pan. Stir fry them for about 2 minutes to heat them through. Season to taste and serve garnished with the sprigs of fresh coriander or parsley.

Pumpkin Purée Enchiladas

Serve these enchiladas with a zero *ProPoints* value crisp green salad.

Serves 4

800 g (1 lb 11 oz) pumpkin or butternut squash, peeled, de-seeded and cut into chunks

a bunch of spring onions, chopped finely

200 g (7 oz) low fat soft cheese with garlic and herbs

1 tablespoon wholegrain Dijon mustard

8 x 25 cm (10 inch) tortilla wraps

400 g can chopped tomatoes

25 g (1 oz) half fat Cheddar cheese, grated

a bunch of fresh coriander, chopped

salt and freshly ground black pepper

4 tablespoons low fat natural yogurt, to serve

9 *ProPoints* values per serving
38 *ProPoints* values per recipe

338 calories per serving

Takes **20 minutes** to prepare,
35 minutes to cook

V

＊ not recommended

1 Steam the pumpkin or squash in a steamer for 15 minutes. If you don't have a steamer, place the pumpkin or squash in a small metal sieve and bring 5 cm (2 inches) of water to the boil in a medium, lidded pan. Suspend the sieve on the edge of the pan so that it hangs down over the boiling water. Put the lid on the pan over the pumpkin and leave to simmer on a medium heat for 15 minutes until the pumpkin is tender.

2 Place the pumpkin in a large mixing bowl with the spring onions, soft cheese and mustard. Mash together and season to taste.

3 Preheat the oven to Gas Mark 4/180°C/fan oven 160°C. Place one of the wraps on the work surface and put a couple of spoonfuls of the pumpkin mixture in the middle of it. Roll up and place, edge side down, in an ovenproof baking dish.

4 Repeat with the other tortillas, laying them side by side in the dish. Tip over the chopped tomatoes and season. Scatter with the grated cheese and coriander and bake for 20 minutes.

5 Serve two tortillas each, topped with a tablespoon of yogurt.

Spicy Bean Burgers

Serves 4

For the bean burgers

calorie controlled cooking spray
1 onion, finely chopped
2 garlic cloves, crushed
1 red chilli, de-seeded and chopped
1 courgette, grated
410 g can cannellini beans, drained and rinsed
1 egg white
grated zest of ½ a lemon
1 tablespoon chopped fresh parsley
½ teaspoon ground cumin
60 g (2 oz) fresh white breadcrumbs
1 tablespoon plain flour
salt and freshly ground black pepper

To serve

4 burger buns
4 tablespoons tomato and chilli relish or tomato relish
a few curly lettuce leaves
1 small red onion, sliced
1 large tomato, sliced

---

7 ProPoints values per serving
30 ProPoints values per recipe

293 calories per serving

Takes **20 minutes** to prepare + **2 hours** chilling, **10 minutes** to cook

V

✳ recommended (at the end of step 2)

1 Heat the cooking spray in a non stick frying pan. Add the onion and cook for 3 minutes until golden, then add the garlic, chilli and courgette and stir fry for 3 minutes until wilted. Set aside to cool slightly.

2 Tip the beans into a food processor, add the egg white, lemon zest, parsley and cumin and blend to a paste. Scrape into a mixing bowl, adding the courgette mixture, breadcrumbs and a generous amount of seasoning. Mix together thoroughly then shape into four burgers. Cover and chill for 2 hours to firm up.

3 Heat a non stick frying pan and spray with the cooking spray. Dust the burgers with the flour and fry the bean burgers for 4–5 minutes on each side.

4 Split and lightly toast the burger buns. Spread one half of each with a spoonful of relish, add some lettuce then top with a bean burger, sliced red onion and tomato. Top with the remaining half burger bun and serve at once.

Cheesy Pasta Bake

A really creamy, cheesy pasta dish with sugar snap peas for crunch.

Serves 4

225 g (8 oz) dried rigatoni
calorie controlled cooking spray
1 red onion, diced
75 g (2¾ oz) baby button mushrooms, quartered
75 g (2¾ oz) sugar snap peas, halved lengthways
125 g (4½ oz) baby spinach leaves, washed
150 g (5½ oz) low fat soft cheese
1 tablespoon torn fresh basil leaves
6 plum tomatoes, sliced
175 g (6 oz) cottage cheese
salt and freshly ground black pepper

8 ProPoints values per serving
31 ProPoints values per recipe

322 calories per serving

Takes **35 minutes** to prepare,
15–20 minutes to cook

V

✳ recommended for up to 1 month

1 Preheat the oven to Gas Mark 4/180°C/fan oven 160°C.

2 Bring a pan of water to the boil, add the pasta and cook for 8 minutes or until al dente.

3 Meanwhile, spray a non stick pan with the cooking spray and cook the onion for 2–3 minutes before adding the mushrooms and sugar snap peas. Cook for 3–4 minutes, stirring occasionally.

4 Drain the pasta and return to the pan with the spinach. Stir around gently to wilt the spinach.

5 Stir in the mushroom and sugar snap pea mixture along with the soft cheese and basil. Stir well to mix, then season.

6 Pour the pasta into an ovenproof dish and top with the tomato slices. Spoon over the cottage cheese and bake in the oven for 15–20 minutes.

Stuffed Jackets

Jacket potatoes are synonymous with Bonfire Night. Topped with this delicious bolognese, you have a quick meal. Serve with a salad of sliced tomatoes and cucumber dressed with 2 tablespoons of fat free salad dressing, for no additional *ProPoints* values.

Serves 8

4 x 225 g (8 oz) baking potatoes
calorie controlled cooking spray
1 onion, chopped
1 red pepper, de-seeded and sliced
2 garlic cloves, chopped
150 g (5½ oz) closed cup mushrooms, sliced
2 x 400 g cans chopped tomatoes
300 g (10½ oz) frozen Quorn mince
1 vegetable stock cube, crumbled
2 teaspoons mixed herbs
2 tablespoons tomato purée
50 g (1¾ oz) half fat Cheddar cheese, grated,
  to serve

4 *ProPoints* values per serving
32 *ProPoints* values per recipe

172 calories per serving

Takes **15 minutes** to prepare,
30 minutes to cook

V

* not recommended

1 Preheat the oven to Gas Mark 5/190°C/fan oven 170°C. Place the potatoes on a baking sheet and bake for 45 minutes until tender.

2 Meanwhile, spray a large pan with the cooking spray and heat until hot. Add the onion and stir fry for 5 minutes until softened. Add the pepper, garlic and mushrooms and continue cooking for another 5 minutes. Stir in the tomatoes, Quorn mince, stock cube, herbs and tomato purée. Bring to the boil, reduce the heat and simmer for 20 minutes, stirring occasionally.

3 Serve the potatoes, one half each, with the mince and topped with the grated cheese.

Vegetable Lasagne

This colourful lasagne makes a delicious meal. Serve with a chopped tomato and onion salad for a colourful, zero **ProPoints** value accompaniment.

Serves 4

1 tablespoon olive oil
1 onion, chopped
1 courgette, sliced
1 red pepper, de-seeded and chopped
1 yellow or green pepper, de-seeded and chopped
225 g (8 oz) mushrooms, sliced
320 g jar tomato pasta sauce
1 teaspoon dried mixed Italian herbs
300 ml (10 fl oz) skimmed milk
25 g (1 oz) plain flour
1 tablespoon low fat spread
50 g (1¾ oz) extra mature Cheddar cheese, grated
125 g (4½ oz) no pre-cook lasagne sheets (6 sheets)
salt and freshly ground black pepper

8 ProPoints values per serving
31 ProPoints values per recipe

340 calories per serving

Takes **20 minutes** to prepare, **45 minutes** to cook

V

✻ recommended

1 Preheat the oven to Gas Mark 5/190°C/fan oven 170°C.

2 Heat the oil in a large frying pan or wok and sauté the onion until softened – about 3–4 minutes. Add the courgette, peppers and mushrooms, and stir fry for another 2 minutes or so. Add the pasta sauce and dried herbs and season. Remove from the heat.

3 To make the cheese sauce, put the milk, flour and low fat spread in a medium saucepan. Bring to the boil, stirring constantly with a wire whisk, until the sauce blends and thickens. Add the cheese and cook gently for about 30 seconds, stirring until melted. Season to taste.

4 Spoon half the vegetable mixture into an oblong ovenproof dish and lay half the lasagne sheets on top. Spread 3–4 tablespoons of the cheese sauce over the lasagne and then add the remaining vegetable mixture. Cover with the rest of the lasagne sheets and spread the rest of the cheese sauce on top.

5 Transfer to the oven and bake for 40–45 minutes, until golden brown.

Variations Vary the vegetables according to your own preferences. For instance, if you're not keen on mushrooms, use a small aubergine instead. The **ProPoints** values will remain the same.

To reduce the **ProPoints** values to 7 per serving, omit the Cheddar cheese from the sauce and sprinkle the surface of the lasagne with 30 g (1¼ oz) of Parmesan cheese, finely grated, just before baking.

Rich Bean Moussaka

A firm favourite, this is delicious served with a zero *ProPoints* value crisp green salad.

Serves 4

calorie controlled cooking spray
1 large aubergine, sliced
1 large onion, chopped
2 garlic cloves, crushed
1 red pepper, de-seeded and chopped
400 g can chopped tomatoes
2 tablespoons tomato purée
215 g can kidney beans, drained, rinsed and mashed gently
½ teaspoon ground cinnamon
4 tablespoons red wine
salt and freshly ground black pepper

For the sauce

4 tablespoons cornflour
600 ml (20 fl oz) skimmed milk
110 g (4 oz) half fat mature Cheddar cheese, grated
1 egg

8 ProPoints values per serving
32 ProPoints values per recipe

312 calories per serving

Takes **50 minutes** to prepare, **1 hour** to cook

V

✷ recommended

1 Preheat the oven to Gas Mark 5/190ºC/fan oven 170ºC. Lightly spray a non stick baking sheet with the cooking spray. Place the aubergine slices on the sheet in one layer. Spray the tops of the aubergine slices with the cooking spray and bake in the oven for 20 minutes or until golden.

2 Meanwhile, spray a large pan with the cooking spray then cook the onion, garlic and pepper for 5 minutes until softened. Add the tomatoes, tomato purée, kidney beans, cinnamon, wine and seasoning. Bring to the boil then simmer for 10 minutes.

3 For the sauce, in a medium saucepan, mix the cornflour with a little of the milk to make a paste. Beat in the remaining milk then cook over a moderate heat, stirring frequently, until thickened. Mix in half the cheese, season to taste, then remove the pan from the heat. Allow the sauce to cool slightly then beat in the egg.

4 Arrange half of the baked aubergine slices in the base of a shallow, ovenproof dish. Spoon over half of the bean mixture then half of the sauce. Repeat the layers, finishing with the sauce. Scatter the remaining cheese over the top.

5 Bake for about an hour, until golden and bubbling.

Tip This dish tastes even better when warmed up the following day as the flavours have had time to develop.

Vegetable Chilli

This chunky stew is flavoured with a tiny amount of chocolate for an authentic Aztec sweetness. Serve with 60 g (2 oz) of dried long grain white rice per person, cooked according to packet instructions, for an additional 6 *ProPoints* values per serving.

Serves 4

4 sun-dried tomatoes
150 ml (5 fl oz) boiling water
calorie controlled cooking spray
2 large onions, chopped
2 garlic cloves, crushed
2 carrots, peeled, quartered lengthways then chopped
1 butternut squash or ½ pumpkin, peeled, de-seeded and cut into 1 cm (½ inch) cubes
2 sweet potatoes, peeled and cubed
1 tablespoon low fat drinking chocolate
2 teaspoons ground cinnamon
1 teaspoon chilli powder (or more to taste)
400 g can chopped tomatoes
300 ml (10 fl oz) vegetable stock
400 g can kidney beans, drained and rinsed
salt and freshly ground black pepper

5 *ProPoints* values per serving
19 *ProPoints* values per recipe

345 calories per serving

Takes **10 minutes** to prepare, **30 minutes** to cook

V

✱ not recommended

1 Place the sun-dried tomatoes in a small bowl and pour the boiling water over. Leave to soak until you need them.

2 Heat a large, lidded, non stick pan and spray with the cooking spray then fry the onions and garlic for 5 minutes until softened, adding a little water if necessary to prevent them from sticking. Add the carrots, squash or pumpkin and sweet potatoes and stir fry for 2 minutes.

3 Drain the sun-dried tomatoes, reserving the soaking liquid, and chop. Add to the vegetable mixture together with their soaking liquid, the chocolate, cinnamon and chilli powder. Stir everything together well. Add the chopped tomatoes and stock and season liberally.

4 Bring to the boil, cover and simmer gently for 20 minutes or until all the vegetables are tender. Finally add the kidney beans and boil rapidly, uncovered, for another 5 minutes until the sauce is rich and thick.

Brown Rice with Chinese Vegetables

Serve this up on a Friday night instead of a Chinese takeaway. It is delicious eaten hot or cold.

Serves 4

225 g (8 oz) dried brown rice
1 vegetable stock cube, crumbled
1 teaspoon Chinese five spice
225 g (8 oz) carrots, peeled and diced
1 red pepper, de-seeded and diced
100 g (3½ oz) mushrooms, sliced
600 ml (20 fl oz) boiling water
100 g (3½ oz) frozen peas
100 g (3½ oz) beansprouts
3 tablespoons soy sauce
2 tablespoons crunchy peanut butter

8 *ProPoints* values per serving
33 *ProPoints* values per recipe

320 calories per serving

Takes **15 minutes** to prepare,
45 minutes to cook

V

✳ recommended

1 Place the rice, stock cube and Chinese five spice in a large lidded pan with 2 tablespoons of water. Cook, stirring, over a low heat for 2 minutes.

2 Add the carrots, pepper and mushrooms and then pour in the boiling water. Bring to the boil, reduce the heat, cover and simmer for 40 minutes, until the liquid has been absorbed and the rice is tender.

3 Add the peas, beansprouts, soy sauce and peanut butter. Stir well, cover again and cook for 5 minutes before serving.

Tip Brown rice takes a lot longer to cook than white but has a deliciously nutty flavour. If you are in a hurry, however, use long grain white rice and cook it for only 20 minutes. The ***ProPoints*** values will remain the same.

Baked Beans and Potato Hash

The whole family will love this cheesy, beany hash.

Serves 4

600 g (1 lb 5 oz) potatoes, peeled and cut into chunks

400 g (14 oz) leeks, washed and sliced

2 garlic cloves, crushed or 2 teaspoons garlic purée

200 g can Weight Watchers from Heinz baked beans

100 g (3½ oz) Gruyère cheese, grated

1 teaspoon dried sage

2 teaspoons vegetable oil

salt and freshly ground black pepper

8 *ProPoints* values per serving
30 *ProPoints* values per recipe

C 310 calories per serving

Takes **30 minutes**

V

✽ recommended

1 Bring a large pan of water to the boil, add the potatoes and cook for 10 minutes. Add the leeks and cook for a further 5 minutes, or until the potatoes are tender. Drain and mash coarsely with the garlic. Stir in the beans, cheese and sage. Season to taste.

2 Heat the oil in a large non stick frying pan and press the potato mixture evenly over the base.

3 Cook for 7–8 minutes, or until crispy and golden on one side. Turn over carefully and cook on the other side for a further 5 minutes. Cut into wedges and serve.

Tip To help turn over the hash, invert the frying pan on to a large plate and then simply slide the hash back into the pan, browned side now facing up.

Something
Special

Special occasions deserve something wonderful, so here are starters and main
course ideas to wow all your family and friends. Surprise them with Celeriac Rosti
with Creamy Roasted Vegetables, Goat's Cheese and Red Onion Tart, Courgette Pots
with Tomato Sauce or Mediterranean Baked Squash.

Delicious recipes for celebrations
or a special meal

Courgette Pots with Tomato Sauce

Serve these lovely little pots as an unusual starter for a special meal.

Serves 4

calorie controlled cooking spray

450 g (1 lb) courgettes, grated

a sprig of fresh rosemary, leaves chopped

2 eggs

200 g (7 oz) low fat soft cheese with garlic and herbs

a kettleful of boiling water

salt and freshly ground black pepper

For the sauce

2 shallots, diced finely

20 cherry tomatoes, halved

1 tablespoon tomato purée

2 *ProPoints* values per serving
10 *ProPoints* values per recipe

C 142 calories per serving

Takes **30 minutes** to prepare,
20–30 minutes to cook

V

* not recommended

1 Preheat the oven to Gas Mark 3/160°C/fan oven 140°C. Base line four ovenproof ramekins with non stick baking parchment and lightly spray with the cooking spray.

2 Spray a large non stick frying pan with the cooking spray and add the courgettes and rosemary. Cook over a low heat, stirring, for 5–7 minutes until beginning to brown and any liquid has evaporated. Set aside to cool slightly.

3 Beat together the eggs and soft cheese in a bowl, then stir into the courgettes. Season and spoon into the ramekins. Place the ramekins in a roasting tin and pour in boiling water to come two thirds of the way up the sides of the ramekins. Bake for 20–30 minutes until set and just golden on top.

4 Meanwhile, make the sauce. Spray a small pan with the cooking spray and heat until hot. Add the shallots and stir fry for 3–4 minutes. Add the tomatoes and cook for 5 minutes with 4 tablespoons of water until mushy. Stir in the tomato purée and season with freshly ground black pepper.

5 To serve, remove the courgette pots from the tin and tip out using an extra plate so that they are cooked side up. Remember to remove the baking parchment. Spoon over the sauce before serving.

Goat's Cheese and Red Onion Tart U(3)U ProPoints value

Surprise your dinner party guests with this stunning dish.

Serves 4

calorie controlled cooking spray

3 red onions, thinly sliced into rings

4 x 15 g filo pastry sheets, measuring 30 x 18 cm
  (12 x 7 inches)

2 heaped teaspoons honey

½ tablespoon fresh thyme, chopped, plus
  4 sprigs to garnish (optional)

75 g (2¾ oz) goat's cheese, sliced

salt and freshly ground black pepper

---

3 ProPoints values per serving
13 ProPoints values per recipe

C **155 calories** per serving

Takes **10 minutes** to prepare,
35 minutes to cook

V

* not recommended

1 Preheat the oven to Gas Mark 5/190°C/fan oven 170°C. Spray four 14 cm (5½ inch) tartlet tins with the cooking spray.

2 Put a lidded non stick frying pan on a low heat and spray with the cooking spray. Add the red onions, cover the pan and cook gently for 20 minutes, stirring occasionally. They should then be very soft but not browned.

3 Cut a sheet of filo pastry into two squares. Spray one with the cooking spray and place the other on top of it, with the corners at angles to each other to make an eight pointed star. Gently press these into a tartlet tin, with the points of the star coming up the sides. Repeat with the other three filo pastry sheets. Spray the tartlets with the cooking spray and bake in the oven for 2–3 minutes until the pastry just starts to turn golden.

4 When the onions are ready, stir in the honey and chopped thyme and season to taste. Divide this mixture between the part cooked tartlets. Top with the goat's cheese and return to the oven for a further 8–10 minutes or until the cheese starts to melt and the pastry is crisp and has turned to a dark golden colour.

5 Remove from the oven and carefully lift the pastry cases on to plates. Garnish with thyme sprigs, if using.

Tip A softer goat's cheese for this recipe gives you a stronger flavour, but a harder goat's cheese often melts and browns better. The choice is yours.

Cold Cucumber and Mint Soup

3 ProPoints value

A luxurious, delicate soup to refresh you on a hot summer's day.

Serves 4

calorie controlled cooking spray
2 small shallots, chopped finely
1 large cucumber, peeled and chopped finely
1 tablespoon plain flour
850 ml (1½ pints) vegetable stock
500 ml (18 fl oz) low fat natural yogurt
a small bunch of fresh mint leaves, chopped
salt and freshly ground black pepper

3 ProPoints values per serving
11 ProPoints values per recipe

C 100 calories per serving

Takes **10 minutes** to prepare + minimum
4 hours chilling, **15 minutes** to cook

V

✱ not recommended

1 Heat a large, lidded, non stick saucepan and spray with the cooking spray. Cook the shallots and cucumber for 5 minutes until softened, adding a little water if necessary to stop the mixture sticking.

2 Blend in the flour and then gradually add the stock, stirring constantly. Season then cover and simmer for 10 minutes.

3 Purée in a liquidiser, cool a little and then stir in the yogurt and mint. Chill until cold before serving.

Tip Do not put the yogurt in while the soup is very hot or it may split.

Variation For a Scandinavian flavour, make with dill rather than mint. The **ProPoints** values will remain the same.

Herby Bean Pâté (Bessara)

This traditional Egyptian recipe tastes as fresh as it looks.

Serves 4

225 g can broad beans, rinsed, drained and skinned
a small bunch of fresh parsley, chopped
a small bunch of fresh coriander, chopped
1 chilli, de-seeded and chopped finely
2 garlic cloves, chopped finely
1½ teaspoons ground cumin
2 tablespoons olive oil
juice of a lemon
salt

To garnish
grated zest of a lemon
1 small red onion, sliced thinly

---

3 ProPoints values per serving
11 ProPoints values per recipe

C **115 calories** per serving

Takes **10 minutes** + chilling

V

✻ not recommended

1 Put all the ingredients, except the garnish, in a food processor with 2 tablespoons of water. Whizz until smooth. If the pâté is too dry, add a little more water.

2 Refrigerate and serve chilled. Garnish with the lemon zest and onion slices.

Variation This is also delicious with sun-dried tomatoes. Stir in 4 finely chopped halves of sun-dried tomatoes that have been soaked in 2 tablespoons of hot water for 30 minutes. The **ProPoints** values will remain the same.

Asparagus and Basil Tart

This makes a lovely early summer dish and is best eaten the day it's made.

1 Preheat the oven to Gas Mark 5/190°C/fan oven 170°C. Bring a large pan of water to the boil. Place a steamer over the pan. Add the asparagus. Cook for 3–5 minutes until just tender. (If you don't have a steamer, cook it in a small amount of boiling water.) Remove from the heat and plunge into cold water to stop it cooking further.

2 Lightly spray a pan with the cooking spray and heat until hot. Add the onions and cook over a low heat until beginning to caramelise, about 8–10 minutes. Set aside to cool slightly.

3 Spray a sheet of filo pastry with the cooking spray. Use to line a 30 x 20 cm (12 x 8 inch) Swiss roll tin. Repeat the layering of the pastry, using the cooking spray and all the sheets.

4 Mix together the onion and eggs and season. Spread over the filo pastry. Top with the asparagus spears, lining them up neatly. Bake for 20 minutes until the pastry is golden and the egg mixture set.

5 Meanwhile, put the pine nut kernels in a dry non stick frying pan and toast for about 2 minutes, tossing constantly until they brown. Serve the tart garnished with the pine nut kernels and basil.

Baked Nutty Stuffed Aubergines

This recipe is filling and oh-so-tasty. Serve with 60 g (2 oz) dried brown rice per person, cooked according to packet instructions, for an extra 6 *ProPoints* values per serving.

Serves 2

1 large aubergine
2 teaspoons extra virgin olive oil
1 onion, chopped finely
2–3 mushrooms, sliced
100 g (3½ oz) Quorn mince
2 tablespoons chopped nuts
1 garlic clove, crushed
1 teaspoon mixed dried herbs
1 teaspoon Marmite
227 g can chopped tomatoes
40 g (1½ oz) half fat Cheddar cheese, grated
salt and freshly ground black pepper
a handful of chopped fresh parsley, to garnish

**7 *ProPoints* values per serving
15 *ProPoints* values per recipe**

C **295 calories** per serving

Takes **30 minutes** to prepare,
30 minutes to cook

V

✻ not recommended

1 Preheat the oven to Gas Mark 6/200°C/fan oven 180°C. Slice the aubergine in half lengthways and then scoop out the flesh, leaving 5 mm (¼ inch) inside the skin to make a firm shell. Chop the flesh finely.

2 Heat the oil in a non stick frying pan and gently fry the aubergine flesh, onion, mushrooms and Quorn mince together for 5 minutes, until soft. Add all the other ingredients apart from the cheese and parsley garnish and mix together.

3 Place the aubergine shells side by side in an ovenproof dish or baking tray and then spoon the mixture equally into each one.

4 Cover the stuffed aubergines with foil and bake in the oven for 20 minutes. Remove the foil, scatter over the cheese and bake for a further 10 minutes, until the cheese is melted and golden. Sprinkle the aubergines with chopped parsley and serve.

Sweet Potato and Red Leicester Strudel

The colour of the sweet potatoes and the Red Leicester cheese makes this a vibrant dish.

Serves 4

450 g (1 lb) sweet potatoes, peeled and diced

75 g (2¾ oz) half fat Red Leicester cheese, grated

1 red pepper, de-seeded and diced

1 onion, chopped finely

4 x 15 g filo pastry sheets, measuring 30 x 18 cm (12 x 7 inches)

1 tablespoon olive oil

salt and freshly ground black pepper

---

6 **ProPoints** values per serving
23 **ProPoints** values per recipe

C 270 **calories** per serving

Takes **40 minutes** to prepare,
20 minutes to cook

V

✱ recommended

1 Bring a large pan of water to the boil, add the sweet potatoes and cook until tender. This will take about 10 minutes.

2 Drain the potatoes and mash them thoroughly. Mix in the cheese, red pepper, onion and seasoning. Allow the mixture to cool for 10 minutes.

3 Preheat the oven to Gas Mark 5/190°C/fan oven 170°C. Brush each sheet of filo pastry lightly with some of the olive oil and stack them one on top of each other. Spread the sweet potato mixture over the top of the stack to within 2 cm (¾ inch) of the edges. Carefully roll up the pastry to enclose the filling.

4 Lift the roll of pastry on to a non stick baking sheet and brush it with the remaining oil. Gently score the top with a sharp knife. Bake for 20 minutes until the pastry is crisp and golden. Cut the strudel into four slices and serve.

Variation Red Leicester cheese has a wonderfully rich, deep orange colour that goes very well with the sweet potato, but you can use half fat Cheddar cheese if you prefer the flavour. The **ProPoints** values will remain the same.

Risotto Primavera

Use whatever zero *ProPoints* value vegetables are in season for this fresh, tasty risotto.

Serves 4

calorie controlled cooking spray
1 onion, chopped
2 garlic cloves, crushed
250 g (9 oz) dried risotto rice
3 tablespoons dry white wine
1 litre (1¾ pints) hot vegetable stock
250 g (9 oz) fresh zero *ProPoints* value vegetables (e.g. baby carrots, baby corn, button mushrooms or asparagus), cut into bite size pieces
salt and freshly ground black pepper
25 g (1 oz) Parmesan cheese, freshly grated, to serve

---

7 *ProPoints* values per serving
29 *ProPoints* values per recipe

C **317 calories** per serving

Takes **40 minutes**

V

✳ not recommended

1 Spray a large non stick pan with the cooking spray and add the onion and garlic. Gently sauté over a medium heat for 5 minutes.

2 Stir in the rice and cook for 1 minute, then add the wine and stir until it is absorbed.

3 Pour in a quarter of the hot stock and stir frequently for about 3 minutes until it is absorbed.

4 Add any firm vegetables, such as carrots. Add the remaining stock a ladleful at a time, stirring frequently until it is absorbed before adding the next ladleful. As you add the stock, add the other vegetables, leaving the most tender (such as asparagus) until the last 5 minutes. It will take 25–30 minutes to add all the stock, by which time the rice should be cooked. If the rice still seems too firm, add a little boiling water and stir until absorbed.

5 Season well and serve as soon as it's ready, topped with the Parmesan cheese.

Broad Bean and Leek Tortilla

This is delicious served with zero *ProPoints* value green vegetables and a fresh tomato salad.

Serves 4

250 g (9 oz) fresh or frozen broad beans
2 leeks, washed, trimmed and sliced
2 courgettes, sliced thinly
1 tablespoon chopped fresh mint (or 1 teaspoon dried)
6 eggs, beaten
75 g (2¾ oz) light mozzarella cheese, cubed
salt and freshly ground black pepper

5 *ProPoints* values per serving
20 *ProPoints* values per recipe

C 240 calories per serving

Takes **20 minutes**

V

✱ not recommended

1 Bring a large pan of water to the boil, add the beans, leeks and courgettes and blanch for 1 minute. Drain and refresh under cold running water, then drain thoroughly. Remove the thick skin of the broad beans to reveal the bright green bean inside.

2 Dry fry the vegetables with the mint in a large, flameproof, non stick frying pan for 2–3 minutes. This will dry off any surplus moisture. Season the eggs and then pour into the pan over the vegetables and cook gently for 6 minutes or until almost set.

3 Preheat the grill. Sprinkle the mozzarella over the top of the tortilla and brown under a hot grill for 2–3 minutes, protecting the pan handle if necessary, until bubbling.

4 Cool slightly, before serving straight from the pan.

Variations If you cannot find light mozzarella, use half fat Cheddar cheese instead. The *ProPoints* values will remain the same.

For a lightly spiced and fruity tortilla, replace the courgette with 1 chopped apple or 25 g (1 oz) of dried apricots, chopped and added in step 2 with 2 teaspoons of mild curry powder. The *ProPoints* values per serving will remain the same.

Celeriac Rosti with Creamy Roasted Vegetables

Rosti make a delicious and low *ProPoints* value base for lots of toppings.

Serves 6

3 yellow peppers, de-seeded and sliced

3 red onions, sliced

700 g (1 lb 9 oz) butternut squash, peeled, de-seeded and cut into chunks

12 garlic cloves, unpeeled

calorie controlled cooking spray

500 g (1 lb 2 oz) celeriac, peeled and grated

500 g (1 lb 2 oz) Desiree potatoes, peeled and grated

150 g (5½ oz) low fat soft cheese with garlic and herbs

3 tablespoons chopped fresh curly parsley

salt and freshly ground black pepper

---

2 *ProPoints* values per serving
15 *ProPoints* values per recipe

C **197 calories** per serving

Takes **20 minutes** to prepare, **40 minutes** to cook

V

* not recommended

1 Preheat the oven to Gas Mark 6/200°C/fan oven 180°C. Place the peppers, onions, squash and garlic cloves in a large roasting dish. Spray with the cooking spray and cook for 40 minutes until tender and beginning to char.

2 Meanwhile, squeeze as much liquid as possible from the grated celeriac and potatoes and dry on kitchen towel. Mix the two together, season and divide into 12 balls.

3 Spray a non stick frying pan with the cooking spray and heat until hot. Place a ball in the pan and flatten with the back of a spatula until very thin. Cook for 5–6 minutes, turning occasionally, until golden and cooked through. You may need to cook these in batches. Remove from the pan and keep warm.

4 Remove the roasting dish from the oven, take out the garlic cloves and squeeze out the soft flesh. Mix with the soft cheese and parsley then stir into the hot roasted vegetables with a little hot water – enough to make a creamy sauce.

5 Serve two rosti each on warm plates topped with the creamy roasted vegetables.

Toasted Courgette and Ricotta Wraps

Impress your guests with these moreish bite size wraps. Make sure you choose large courgettes since they're easier to work with.

Serves 4

4 large courgettes, trimmed
2 tablespoons olive oil
3 shallots, finely chopped
1 garlic clove, crushed
2 tomatoes, skinned, de-seeded and diced
200 g (7 oz) ricotta cheese
1 egg, beaten
25 g (1 oz) fresh wholemeal breadcrumbs
1 tablespoon fresh basil, roughly torn
15 g (½ oz) Parmesan cheese, grated
salt and freshly ground black pepper

1 Slice the courgettes horizontally to make long thin strips. Bring a large pan of water to the boil, add the courgette strips and cook for 2 minutes to soften them. Drain on sheets of double thickness kitchen towel.

2 Heat 1 tablespoonful of oil in a lidded non stick pan and add the shallots and garlic. Cover and cook over a low heat for 10 minutes, until very soft but not browned. Preheat the oven to Gas Mark 5/190°C/fan oven 170°C.

3 Remove the pan from the heat and add the tomatoes, ricotta cheese, egg, breadcrumbs, basil and seasoning. Mix together thoroughly, then take spoonfuls of the mixture and place on one end of each courgette strip and roll up, enclosing the filling.

4 Lift the courgette wraps on to a non stick baking sheet, brush with the remaining oil and sprinkle with the Parmesan cheese. Bake for 15–20 minutes, until piping hot.

5 ProPoints values per serving
20 ProPoints values per recipe

230 calories per serving

Takes **20 minutes** to prepare,
20 minutes to cook

V

✻ recommended

Tip You can eat these tasty wraps hot or cold, they're delicious either way.

Fresh Pasta with Creamy Watercress Sauce

Watercress has a fantastic peppery taste and goes perfectly with pasta in this creamy sauce.

Serves 4

400 g (14 oz) dried pasta shapes
calorie controlled cooking spray
4 garlic cloves, sliced finely
175 g (6 oz) watercress, washed
 and chopped roughly
150 g (5½ oz) low fat soft cheese

grated zest from ½ a lemon
1 teaspoon dried chilli flakes
 (optional)
150 ml (5 fl oz) skimmed milk
salt and freshly ground black
 pepper

1 Bring a large pan of water to the boil, add the pasta and cook according to the packet instructions until al dente.

2 Meanwhile, spray a large lidded frying pan with the cooking spray and fry the garlic slices until golden. Add the watercress and cover the pan for a few minutes, stirring occasionally until wilted.

3 Add the soft cheese, lemon zest, seasoning, chilli flakes (if using), milk and the drained pasta with a few tablespoons of the pasta cooking liquid. Gently fold together and serve.

*11 **ProPoints** values per serving
45 **ProPoints** values per recipe*

C **350 calories** per serving

Takes **15 minutes**

V

* not recommended

Blue Cheese and Broccoli Soufflés ⓤ③ⓤ

These soufflés really work and the secret is baking them twice, so give them a go. Serve with a zero *ProPoints* value green salad and a handful of cherry tomatoes.

Serves 4

calorie controlled cooking spray
110 g (4 oz) broccoli, chopped
15 g (½ oz) low fat spread
1 garlic clove, crushed
25 g (1 oz) plain flour
175 ml (6 fl oz) skimmed milk
2 eggs, separated
40 g (1½ oz) Danish blue cheese
1 egg white
salt and freshly ground black pepper

ⓒ 3 *ProPoints* values per serving
13 *ProPoints* values per recipe

C 140 **calories** per serving

🕐 Takes **20 minutes** to prepare,
45 minutes to cook + cooling

V

✱ not recommended

1 Preheat the oven to Gas Mark 4/180°C/fan oven 160°C. Spray 4 x 200 ml (7 fl oz) ovenproof ramekins with the cooking spray.

2 Bring a small pan of water to the boil, add the broccoli and cook for 5 minutes until tender. Drain well and mash.

3 Melt the low fat spread in a saucepan, add the garlic and flour and cook, stirring, for 1 minute until the mixture forms a ball. Remove from the heat and gradually add the milk, stirring until smooth after each addition. Return to the heat and cook over a low heat, stirring continuously until thickened. Season. Cool slightly before beating in the egg yolks, broccoli and cheese.

4 In a clean, grease-free bowl, whisk the egg white until stiff. Add a spoonful to the broccoli mix to slacken it and then carefully fold in the broccoli mix to the remaining white. Spoon the mixture into the ramekins.

5 Place the ramekins in a roasting tin filled with sufficient hot water to come about a third of the way up the sides of the dishes. Bake for 20 minutes until puffed up and golden on top. Remove from the oven and allow the roasting tin to cool. They will sink at this point. When cool, loosen and then tip out, cooked side up, on to a baking sheet lined with non stick baking parchment.

6 For the second baking, preheat the oven to Gas Mark 4/180°C/fan oven 160°C. Cook the soufflés for 25 minutes until puffed up again. Serve immediately.

Tip Make these up to 24 hours in advance. Cook once, cool and then remove from the ramekins. Cover and refrigerate until required.

Spinach and Mushroom Roulade

This recipe can be served as a main course with a hot tomato sauce and new potatoes, remembering to add the **ProPoints** values, or it serves 6 people as a starter for 2 **ProPoints** values per serving.

Serves 4

calorie controlled cooking spray
350 g (12 oz) fresh spinach, washed
4 eggs, separated
freshly grated nutmeg
350 g (12 oz) mushrooms, chopped roughly
2 garlic cloves, crushed
200 g (7 oz) low fat soft cheese
1 tablespoon skimmed milk
1 tablespoon snipped fresh chives
salt and freshly ground black pepper

3 **ProPoints** values per serving
13 **ProPoints** values per recipe

C **172 calories** per serving

Takes **30 minutes** + cooling

V

✳ not recommended

1 Preheat the oven to Gas Mark 4/180°C/fan oven 160°C.

2 Lightly grease a 23 x 33 cm (9 x 13 inch) Swiss roll tin with the cooking spray and line with non stick baking parchment.

3 Place the spinach in a large lidded pan, without adding any liquid. Cover and cook for 2 minutes until wilted, then drain well, squeezing out the excess liquid.

4 Chop the spinach and place in a bowl, then mix in the beaten egg yolks. In a separate, grease-free bowl, whisk the egg whites until they form soft peaks. Stir a spoonful of egg whites into the spinach to slacken the mixture then gently fold in the remainder, adding nutmeg and seasoning. Pour into the prepared tin and level the surface.

5 Bake for 10–12 minutes until set and slightly springy to the touch. Turn out on to a sheet of non stick baking parchment, leave the lining paper on and cover with a clean tea towel to keep the roulade moist as it cools.

6 Meanwhile, lightly coat a lidded non stick pan with the cooking spray, add the mushrooms, garlic and seasoning, and cook, covered, for 3 minutes or until juicy.

7 Uncover the pan and cook for a further 2–3 minutes until the juices have evaporated. Spread out on a plate and leave to cool. Mix the soft cheese with the milk and chives.

8 Peel the lining paper away from the roulade and gently spread the cream cheese mixture all over. Scatter the garlic mushrooms over evenly, then, with a long side towards you, roll up the roulade, using the baking parchment to help you. Cut into slices to serve.

Vegetable Pie

The vermouth in the filling and the attractive filo pastry top turn a vegetable pie into something a little different.

Serves 4

350 g (12 oz) baby new potatoes, halved
175 g (6 oz) baby carrots, scrubbed and trimmed
225 g (8 oz) broad beans
2 leeks, washed and sliced
100 g (3½ oz) frozen peas
400 g can chopped tomatoes
1 tablespoon dried mixed herbs
2 tablespoons vermouth
4 x 45 g filo pastry sheets, measuring (50 x 25 cm) (20 x 10 inches)
25 g (1 oz) low fat spread, melted
salt and freshly ground black pepper

1 Preheat the oven to Gas Mark 6/200°C/fan oven 180°C.

2 Bring a large pan of water to the boil, add the potatoes and carrots and cook for 10 minutes.

3 Add the beans, leeks and peas. Bring back to the boil and simmer for a further 5 minutes.

4 Drain the vegetables and toss with the chopped tomatoes, herbs, vermouth and seasoning. Spoon into a large ovenproof dish.

5 In turn, brush each sheet of pastry with the low fat spread and loosely crumple it up. Place on top of the vegetables. Arrange the pastry so that all the vegetables are covered.

6 Bake for 20 minutes, until the pastry is crisp and golden.

8 ProPoints values per serving
32 ProPoints values per recipe

C **344 calories** per serving

Takes **30 minutes** to prepare,
20 minutes to cook

V

✱ recommended

Squash Tagine with Apricot Couscous

8 ProPoints value

Serves 4

calorie controlled cooking spray
2 onions, chopped finely
2 garlic cloves, crushed
1 tablespoon harissa paste
1 teaspoon ground cumin
350 ml (12 fl oz) hot vegetable stock
3 tomatoes, chopped
150 g (5½ oz) whole green beans

500 g (1 lb 2 oz) butternut squash, peeled, de-seeded and cut into chunks
400 g can chick peas, drained and rinsed
50 g (1¾ oz) ready to eat apricots, chopped finely
grated zest and juice of ½ a lemon
200 g (7 oz) dried couscous
4 tablespoons chopped fresh coriander
salt and freshly ground black pepper

1 Heat a large lidded saucepan and spray with the cooking spray. Gently fry the onions and garlic for 5 minutes until softened but not browned. Stir in the harissa and cumin and cook for 1 minute.

2 Add 75 ml (3 fl oz) of the stock, the tomatoes, green beans and butternut squash. Season. Turn down the heat, cover and simmer for 15 minutes. Add the chick peas and cook for another 30 minutes.

3 Meanwhile, add the chopped apricots, lemon juice and zest to the remaining stock and pour this over the couscous. Cover and leave to stand for 5 minutes. Fluff up with a fork and stir in half of the coriander. Serve the tagine with the couscous, sprinkled with the remaining coriander.

8 ProPoints values per serving
31 ProPoints values per recipe

295 calories per serving

Takes **10 minutes** to prepare, **1 hour** to cook

V

✱ recommended

Stilton Mushroom Filo Parcels

Try serving these delicious filo parcels with a zero *ProPoints* value green salad.

Serves 6

calorie controlled cooking spray

750 g (1 lb 10 oz) mixed mushrooms, chopped finely

6 spring onions, sliced

3 fresh thyme sprigs, leaves only

2 garlic cloves, crushed

150 g (5½ oz) Stilton cheese, crumbled

12 x 15 g filo pastry sheets, measuring 30 x 18 cm (12 x 7 inches)

2 teaspoons caraway seeds (optional)

freshly ground black pepper

---

5 *ProPoints* values per serving
29 *ProPoints* values per recipe

212 calories per serving

Takes **20 minutes** to prepare,
30 minutes to cook

V

✳ not recommended

1 Preheat the oven to Gas Mark 6/200°C/fan oven 180°C.

2 Spray a non stick frying pan with the cooking spray and heat until hot. Add the mushrooms, spring onions, thyme and garlic and cook over a high heat for 5–7 minutes. The mushrooms should release their juices, which will then evaporate. Remove from the heat.

3 Crumble in the cheese and mix to combine. Season with black pepper (the Stilton will make the mixture salty enough).

4 Lay a sheet of pastry on a board, spray with the cooking spray and top with another sheet. Spoon a sixth of the mixture into the middle, fold over two opposites sides of pastry and roll up to make a parcel. Spray with the cooking spray and sprinkle with the caraway seeds, if using. Repeat to make six parcels. Place on a non stick baking sheet and bake for 20–25 minutes until golden.

Variation If you don't like blue cheese, try using the same amount of Cheddar cheese instead, for the same *ProPoints* values per serving.

Chicory Gratin

This recipe for chicory baked in a cheese sauce is simple to prepare and the usually bitter heads of chicory become sweet and caramelised.

Serves 4

50 g (1¾ oz) low fat spread
8 chicory bulbs
50 g (1¾ oz) plain flour
600 ml (20 fl oz) skimmed milk
100 g (3½ oz) low fat soft cheese
1 tablespoon French mustard
50 g (1¾ oz) mature Cheddar cheese, grated
salt and freshly ground black pepper

6 *ProPoints* values per serving
24 *ProPoints* values per recipe

C **249 calories** per serving

Takes **10 minutes** to prepare,
50 minutes to cook

V

✱ not recommended

1 Melt the low fat spread in a large, lidded, non stick frying pan then add the chicory, turning to coat. Season, cover with a piece of baking parchment tucked down the sides of the pan and cover with a lid. Sweat over the lowest possible heat for 35 minutes until tender and caramelised.

2 Remove the chicory heads from the pan with a slotted spoon and place in an ovenproof dish, packing them tightly together. Preheat the oven to Gas Mark 5/190°C/fan oven 170°C.

3 Put the flour in the pan used for the chicory and cook for 30 seconds, then add the milk a little at a time, whisking between additions to make a smooth sauce. Add half the soft cheese, mustard and seasoning and stir until smooth over a gentle heat.

4 Pour the sauce over the chicory, sprinkle the remaining cheese on top and bake for 15 minutes until bubbling and golden.

Sunday Roast with Parsley Sauce

U8U ProPoints value

Enjoy a delicious Sunday roast with family or friends.

Serves 4

For the roast

1 tablespoon sunflower oil
1 onion, chopped finely
1 garlic clove, crushed
350 g (12 oz) vegetarian mince
1 tablespoon soy sauce
175 g (6 oz) carrots, peeled and grated
1 teaspoon dried mixed herbs
225 g can baked beans in tomato sauce
50 g (1¾ oz) fresh breadcrumbs
1 egg, beaten
salt and freshly ground black pepper

For the sauce

425 ml (15 fl oz) skimmed milk
25 g (1 oz) low fat spread
25 g (1 oz) cornflour
4 tablespoons chopped fresh parsley

---

8 ProPoints values per serving
30 ProPoints values per recipe

391 calories per serving

Takes **30 minutes** to prepare,
1 hour to cook

V

✳ recommended (roast only)

1 Preheat the oven to Gas Mark 4/180°C/fan oven 160°C. Line a 900 g (2 lb) loaf tin with non stick baking parchment.

2 Heat the oil in a frying pan and add the onion, garlic and mince. Stir fry for 5 minutes.

3 Stir in the soy sauce, carrots, herbs and baked beans and cook for a further 2 minutes.

4 Transfer everything to a large mixing bowl and add the breadcrumbs, beaten egg and seasoning. Use a potato masher to mash all the ingredients together. Spoon the mixture into the prepared tin, levelling it with the back of a spoon, and bake in the oven for 1 hour.

5 To make the sauce, heat the milk until just boiling. Melt the low fat spread in a medium saucepan and then remove it from the heat and stir in the cornflour to make a paste. Pour the hot milk over the paste and whisk well. Return the mixture to the heat and cook, stirring, until you have a smooth, thickened sauce. Stir in the chopped parsley and season to taste.

6 Carefully remove the cooked loaf from the tin and peel away the lining paper. Cut it into thick slices and drizzle with a little of the parsley sauce.

Tip Keep parsley in the freezer; rub it between your hands while it is still frozen and it will be ready to use.

Portobello Mushrooms with Rice Noodles

3 ProPoints value

These not only taste great they also look very impressive for a dinner party.

Serves 4

8 portobello mushrooms
200 ml (7 fl oz) vegetable stock
600 ml (20 fl oz) boiling water
125 g (4½ oz) dried very fine stir fry rice noodles
calorie controlled cooking spray
2 cm (¾ inch) fresh root ginger, chopped
2 garlic cloves, crushed
2 spring onions, sliced
1 large courgette, grated
1 large carrot, peeled and grated
2 tablespoons soy sauce

3 ProPoints values per serving
13 ProPoints values per recipe

C **96 calories** per serving

Takes **40 minutes**

V

✳ recommended for up to **1 month**

1 Place the mushrooms in a large lidded pan with the stock (you may have to do this in two batches). Bring the stock to the boil, cover the pan and simmer for 5–6 minutes until the mushrooms are cooked. Remove them with a slotted spoon and keep warm.

2 Top up the stock with the boiling water and place the rice noodles in the pan (off the heat). Leave to stand for 4 minutes.

3 Meanwhile, heat a non stick frying pan or wok, spray with the cooking spray and stir fry the ginger, garlic and spring onions for 2 minutes. Add the grated courgette and carrot and continue to stir fry for another 2 minutes.

4 Stir in the drained noodles and soy sauce and cook for 1 minute.

5 Place the mushrooms on a serving plate and, using a spoon and fork, pick up a small amount of the noodles and coil them around the fork. Place the coiled noodles on top of a mushroom. Repeat this on the remaining mushrooms, spooning any juices or vegetables over the noodles. Serve immediately.

Mediterranean Baked Squash

Butternut squash acts as a great container for a filling, and of course you can eat the whole thing, skin included. Serve with a zero *ProPoints* value mixed salad.

Serves 6

850 ml (1½ pints) vegetable stock

200 g (7 oz) dried brown rice

3 x 600 g (1 lb 5 oz) butternut squash, cut in half and de-seeded

16 cherry tomatoes, quartered

125 g (4½ oz) black olives in brine, drained and halved

6 roasted peppers in brine, drained and chopped roughly

2 teaspoons dried thyme

4 tablespoons tomato purée

freshly ground black pepper

---

4 *ProPoints* values per serving
27 *ProPoints* values per recipe

274 calories per serving

Takes **10 minutes** to prepare,
1 hour 15 minutes to cook

V

* not recommended

1 In a large lidded pan, bring the stock to the boil, then add the rice. Bring back to the boil, cover, reduce to a simmer and cook for 25 minutes until tender. Check occasionally, adding more water if boiling dry, so that almost all the stock has been absorbed by the end.

2 Meanwhile, preheat the oven to Gas Mark 4/180°C/fan oven 160°C. Place the squash skin side down in a large ovenproof dish. Pour 150 ml (5 fl oz) of water in the bottom of the dish and bake for 20 minutes.

3 In a pan, mix together the cooked rice, tomatoes, olives, peppers, thyme and tomato purée. Season with black pepper.

4 Remove the squash from the oven, spoon the rice mixture into the squash, cover with foil and bake for 40–50 minutes until the squash is tender. Remove from the pan and serve hot.

Roasted Vegetables with Brie and Wine Sauce

A superb treat.

Serves 2

6 spring onions

1 fennel bulb, cut into chunks

2 white chicory bulbs, halved lengthways

6 baby carrots, scrubbed and trimmed

2 banana shallots or large regular shallots, halved

150 g (5½ oz) new potatoes, scrubbed

2 fresh thyme sprigs

4 garlic cloves, unpeeled

calorie controlled cooking spray

110 g (4 oz) Brie, chopped roughly

3 tablespoons white wine

2 teaspoons fresh thyme leaves

freshly ground black pepper

7 *ProPoints* values per serving
15 *ProPoints* values per recipe

347 calories per serving

Takes **15 minutes** to prepare,
40 minutes to cook

V

✳ not recommended

1 Preheat the oven to Gas Mark 6/200°C/fan oven 180°C. Place all the vegetables in a large roasting tin with the thyme sprigs and garlic and spray with the cooking spray.

2 Roast in the oven for 40 minutes until tender and beginning to char.

3 To make the sauce, place the Brie, wine and thyme leaves in a small pan set over a low heat. Stir until melted. Remove the roasting tin from the oven. Pop the roasted garlic cloves from their skins. Mash with a fork. Add to the cheese sauce.

4 Season the vegetables with black pepper and serve the sauce in a dipping pot with the roasted vegetables.

Nut Loaf with Roast Garlic and Tomato Sauce

Serves 4

calorie controlled cooking spray
2 courgettes, coarsely grated
100 g (3½ oz) mix of nuts (e.g. walnuts, almonds, cashews), ground in a food processor or chopped finely
2 garlic cloves, crushed
grated zest of ½ a lemon
50 g (1¾ oz) fresh breadcrumbs
400 g can artichoke hearts in brine, rinsed, drained and chopped
1 teaspoon dried sage or a small bunch of fresh sage, chopped
1 egg white
1 tablespoon tomato purée
1 tablespoon soy sauce
salt and freshly ground black pepper

For the sauce
8 garlic cloves, unpeeled
450 g (1 lb) tomatoes, quartered
1 tablespoon balsamic vinegar

5 ProPoints values per serving
21 ProPoints values per recipe

260 calories per serving

Takes **20 minutes** to prepare,
45 minutes to cook

V

✱ recommended (uncooked)

1 Preheat the oven to Gas Mark 6/200°C/fan oven 180°C and spray a large sheet of foil with the cooking spray.

2 Put all the remaining nut roast ingredients in a large bowl, season and mix together well. Tip the mixture into the centre of the foil and shape into a fat sausage about 25 cm (10 inches) long and 10 cm (4 inches) wide, packing it tightly. Roll the sausage in the foil and place on a baking sheet. Roast for 30 minutes and then unwrap the foil and roast for a further 15 minutes, until browned.

3 Meanwhile, make the sauce. Place the garlic cloves and tomatoes in a baking tray, season and sprinkle with the balsamic vinegar. Roast alongside the nut roast.

4 After about 30 minutes, when the tomatoes and garlic are brown on the edges, remove from the oven. Allow to cool for 10 minutes and then pinch the garlic cloves to remove the papery skins. Liquidise the tomatoes and garlic and any juices in the tray and check the seasoning. Slice the roast and serve hot with the sauce.

Bulgar Wheat Pilaff

Bulgar wheat has a satisfying texture and makes an interesting change from potatoes or rice. It is a great accompaniment to many of the recipes in this book.

Serves 4

25 g (1 oz) pine nut kernels
25 g (1 oz) flaked almonds
calorie controlled cooking spray
1 onion, chopped
225 g (8 oz) bulgar wheat
600 ml (20 fl oz) chicken stock
50 g (1½ oz) raisins, sultanas or currants
a small bunch of fresh coriander or mint, chopped
salt and freshly ground black pepper

8 ProPoints values per serving
33 ProPoints values per recipe

315 calories per serving

Takes **5 minutes** to prepare + **10 minutes** standing time, **40 minutes** to cook

V

✳ not recommended

1 Toast the pine nut kernels and almonds in a dry frying pan.

2 Spray a lidded non stick pan with the cooking spray and fry the onion for 4 minutes or until soft. Add a tablespoon of water if it sticks.

3 Stir in the bulgar wheat and cook for a further 4 minutes, stirring all the time. Add the stock, bring to the boil and stir. Then reduce the heat, cover and simmer for 20 minutes until all the liquid is absorbed.

4 Season, add the other ingredients, including the toasted pine nut kernels and almonds and place a sheet of baking parchment over the pan. Replace the lid and allow to stand for 10 minutes. Fluff up with a fork before serving.

Index